Written by two acclaimed journalists (Franklin won a Pulitzer Prize for his articles on shocktrauma), this book takes you into the futuristic world of healing for a graphic, minute-by-minute account of the struggle to reverse the tide of violent death.

"[A] REALISTIC DRAMA, AS IN-FORMATIVE AS IT IS INTRIGUING ...FILLED WITH RUTHLESS POL-ITICS, PROFESSIONAL JEALOUSY, LIFE-AND-DEATH CRISES."

Los Angeles Times

"ENGROSSING."

The Chattanooga Times

SHOCKTRAUMA

Jon Franklin
and
Alan Doelp

FAWCETT CREST • NEW YORK

Foreword

TRAUMA IS A DISEASE THAT FINGERPAINTS ITS
signature in blood and brain; this is not a book for the
timid. It is a work of painstakingly documented non-
fiction, the product of five years of research, accurate
in fact and context.

This book began in 1974 when our journalistic curi-
osity was aroused by local physicians who, always off
the record, complained bitterly about the Maryland Institute for Emergency Medical Services and the man
who built it. The complaints focused on charges of empire building and patient-stealing, and there were *sotto
voce* allegations of too-aggressive medicine being practiced there.

R Adams Cowley, in contrast, talked openly and on
the record. He answered our questions bluntly and honestly and gave us unrestricted access to Shocktrauma
(as the institute is familiarly called). He asked only that
we respect his patients' privacy, and we have complied
by carefully disguising not only the patients but also the
medical personnel who treated them. The exceptions,

James P. Mause, Reese D. Loftin and Charles A. "Dutch" Ruppersberger 3d, gave us permission to cite their cases.

One detail of Cowley's personal history requires mention here, if only to mollify the occasional unemployed copyreader who picks up this book. When the complete name R Adams Cowley is used, the omission of a period after the R is no accident. It is not an oversight on the part of the authors, editors, copyreaders or typographers of this book. The blame lies with Alta Adams Cowley, the heart surgeon's mother.

Her father was Rufus Adams, a forceful gentleman of the traditional Mormon school, who insisted in 1917 that the new baby be named after him. Alta pointed out that Rufus was such an awful name that even Rufus himself signed with an initial only. But Grandfather Adams persisted, offering to bribe Alta with a brand-new wicker baby buggy. She gave in but when the time came to fill in the birth certificate she couldn't do it. She wrote down "R" instead and, as a result, R-*no-period-please* Adams Cowley's life has been plagued by a progression of disbelieving registrars, paymasters, secretaries, bureaucrats and reporters. His friends call him "R A.," and his four brothers just call him "R."

As with any undertaking of this magnitude we depended on the cooperation of innumerable persons whose help we would, at the risk of leaving someone out, gratefully acknowledge. Dr. Cowley and Elizabeth Scanlan, of course, were invaluable in providing the medical and historical framework. Others of the Cowley group, including Sandy Bond, John Ashworth and Marianna Herschel, supplied additional vital information.

FOREWORD

Persons outside the shocktrauma unit helped broaden our perspective and clarify the issues. We gratefully acknowledge the assistance of Dr. David R. Boyd, Dr. Benjamin H. Trump, Brig. Gen. Sam F. Seeley, USA (ret.), Dr. John H. Moxley 3d, Dr. G. Robert Mason, Dr. John B. DeHoff and Dr. J. Tyson Tildon. Also, former Maryland Governor Marvin Mandel, his chief of staff Frank A. DeFilippo and his aide Frederick L. Dewberry, along with several other individuals whose names we promised not to reveal.

The stressful nature of Shocktrauma work guarantees a high turnover rate, and many of the persons mentioned here have since moved on. Dr. T. Crawford McAslan is now at Baltimore City Hospital, and Dr. Nathan Schnaper is chairman of the psychiatric branch at the Baltimore Cancer Research Center. We thank them both for the help they gave us.

Other current and former Shocktrauma staffers upon whom we relied were Dr. Alasdair K. Conn, Dr. Sandy Kuehl, Dr. Mike Carr, Dr. Dermot P. Byrnes, Dr. Roy A. M. Myers, Dr. William Gill and Dr. Howard Champion.

Among Shocktrauma nurses, our thanks to Patty Hurn, Barbara Friend, Mary Murphy, Lynne Toth, Jo Walrath, Denise Cost, Nadine Jacobs, Debby Buckmaster, Tom Baker, Pam Bell and especially to Janet Ward. The orderlies and attendants were also helpful, among them most notably Wally Price.

On the literary end of the project, we dare not overlook our considerable debt to Jo Bruen, George Rodgers, Kelly Gilbert and the ghost of G. Vern Blasdell,

FOREWORD

or to Jay Acton and Denis Holler, and our excellent editor at St. Martin's, Les Pockell.

But most of all we are obligated to "Tex" and "Freckles," who showed us what Shocktrauma was really about, and why.

Jon Franklin
Alan Doelp
Baltimore, 1979

1

THE NIGHT IS MOONLESS AND A GLACIAL WIND
howls across Middle River, rocking the state police helicopter. As the pilot works down his checklist the medic
settles into the left seat and snaps his shoulder harness.
Slowly the rotors grind around once, twice, three times
and the jet engine catches. The pilot flexes his cold
fingers and wraps them around the joy stick. His lips
move against the black plastic radio microphone.

Thirty miles away a Ford compact lies wheels-up at
the bottom of a steep embankment. A dozen cars are
stopped near the broken guard rail and flashlights play
over the splintered pines, the scooped-out earth, the
shards of glass and the torn scraps of thin metal. Below,
in the laurel underbrush, two ambulance crewmen and
a state trooper use a pry bar to open the front door.

The thicket limits the door's motion, but eighteen
inches is enough to allow the trooper to pull a dazed
teenaged girl from the wreckage. The girl fights the
trooper's hands, tries to stand on her own, staggers,

trips on a splintered oak branch and falls into the ambulance driver, who lowers her onto the waiting stretcher. She tells the driver that her brother is still in the car. Her voice is high and tinny. "My dad's going to kill me," she says.

Already the other ambulance crewman has wormed his way into the car and is attempting to free the boy, who is pinned against the windshield by the weight of the seat. But in the confined space the man can't find the leverage he needs and he curses as he slips, slicing his own hand on the shattered windshield. His blood mixes with the sticky flow that pumps from the boy's forehead and cascades onto the sun visor. The flashlight beam catches the ivory white of bare skull. The man calls for pressure bandages.

At Glenn L. Martin airport, the jet howls and the skids grind against concrete as the rotors catch and lift. The yellow and white machine moves tentatively away from its pad, testing the air, nose depressed, lights blinking, gaining forward speed, climbing above the chain-link fence and dirt road. The hard streetlights of eastern Baltimore County stretch below. Headlights move along the streets of the city.

The crackling voice in the pilot's ears tells him the helicopter is cleared for a straight flight. The old Huey rattles and groans and the heater blows cold. It was built for the tropics, and the army mechanics patched two small round holes in its tail before turning it over to the Maryland State Police. Now as it scoots above the city, the Huey is embedded in the February night. The air in the cockpit is so cold it burns. Water vapor blows from the medic's nostrils. Below passes a familiar landmark, a drive-in screen that both medevac technicians drive past every day on their way home. Since November the marquee has said FANTASTA and TORTURED MAIDENS with CARTOONS.

Two thousand feet above a tank farm, as the helicopter bounces and twists in the turbulent air, the pilot's finger points through the Plexiglass. The medic nods. He sees it too.

Far across the glittering city and the black water, ice-blue emergency lights stand out, flashing. Police, firefighters and rescue crews are still converging on the accident scene and several vehicles, including a fire engine, are caught in the line of traffic that is already beginning to back up as the troopers block off three lanes with a ring of flares. Volunteers direct the cars slowly, one at a time, across the median. As the Huey approaches, it passes over an ambulance speeding toward Community Hospital with the teenaged girl.

As the helicopter swings wide around the circle of flares two sets of eyes peer intently through the Plexiglass, searching for the nightmare wires that, unseen, could send the Huey spinning to the earth in flames. Both men point as the landing lights sweep across a run of high-tension towers. The pilot approaches the ground from the opposite direction, swinging his craft around at the last moment to avoid those clawing wires.

In the thick underbrush, two firemen strain to hold the Ford's seat up while a third pulls the driver free. The right leg of the boy's light tan jeans is wet with blood.

Bystanders shield their eyes as the helicopter touches pavement, filling the air with the blowing grit. The

3

medic runs beneath the rotors, a folding stretcher in his left hand and an equipment box in his right. A fireman with a flashlight wand beckons traffic to keep it moving.

Beside the overturned Ford, the helicopter medic immediately assumes command, curtly ordering the ambulance attendant to slit the bloody trouser leg. The attendant frowns, hesitates, and opens his mouth to object, but the medic has already turned away. While the attendant kneels by the bloody leg, the medic, still in his flight helmet, inserts a hard plastic airway device between the boy's teeth and into his throat.

With his thumb, the medic peels back the boy's left eyelid and shines a light into the eye. The pupil contracts quickly. The right eye reacts the same way. There is still time.

Four men carry the stretcher beneath the rotors, the medic holding a bottle of Ringer's lactate above the blanket-covered form. The patient goes into the rear of the cockpit and the medic crawls in beside him and swings the door shut. The jet screams in response to the pilot's rapidly-moving hands and the blades bite into the night air as the helicopter lurches back into its element, away from the wires, away from the ground, away from the headlights moving across the median, away from the overturned Ford, from the guttering ring of flares. On the ground, ears hurt in the silence the jet leaves behind.

The Huey flies at 120 miles an hour as the medic pumps oxygen through the plastic mouthpiece and into the boy's lungs. He evaluates the situation, taking note of the huge turban of bandages that covers the head from the eyes up and of the inflatable plastic splint the

4

ambulance attendant has put on the right leg. Finally, the aircraft's heater grows warm.

The medic shines his light again into the unconscious eyes. The pupils contract more slowly now and the question is time—time and blood loss. The boy has spilled so much oxygen-carrying blood that the delicate cells of his brain are beginning to suffocate. In the language of medicine, the patient is slipping deeply into shock. The Huey bucks and wallows in the clear, cold air, and the second hand on the instrument panel clock sweeps around once, twice, three times.

Finally the University of Maryland Hospital complex appears in the distance. Landing lights cut through blowing wisps of icy fog as the aircraft drops quickly toward the spotlighted roof of a parking garage. As the skids reach for the big red X painted on the concrete, an ambulance crawls out of the parking ramp and stops. A nurse, an anesthesiologist and two attendants run, heads down, beneath the rotors.

The transfer is completed quickly, and when the ambulance is gone the pilot lifts the Huey, banks to port, rises above an ancient cemetery, circles and heads east in a gentle climb over Baltimore harbor. A forty-story building falls below, to the left, and two tugboats push on the side of a freighter. To the north the flash-flash-flash of a police car emergency blinker stands out among the thousands of soft yellow street lights that mark the avenues of the city.

Wind buffets the aircraft. The instruments glow red. The Huey was designed for Vietnam, but it performs well for the urban bush pilot and his medic partner. The medic leans back and wriggles his toes in front of the heater vent. He rolls his head and looks up, through the plastic overhead, through the spinning rotors, into the inky sky.

A dispatcher's voice crackles in the pilot's ear and the medic reaches for a notepad and map. The helicopter banks sharply to starboard and heads west, nose down, toward the Appalachians.

2

"WE BRING THEM IN THIS WAY," SAYS COWLEY, walking slowly down the long, dingy hallway in the basement beneath the old hospital. Automatically pushing through a succession of heavy double doors, he follows a wide red line painted on the tile floor. The final doors open into the Maryland Institute for Emergency Medical Services. Suddenly the environment becomes bright and clean. In the background, an air compressor chugs.

The red line runs to a waiting elevator, but the way is blocked by a battered yellow sign. Rather than summon the second elevator, Cowley turns toward the stairwell. As he walks, he talks of death with intimate familiarity, with the authority of a general who knows his enemy well.

"You think people die from accidents or heart attacks, but they really don't. Not directly. Those things produce shock, which is sluggish or nonexistent circulation, and that's what kills you. Shock . . . think of it as a pause in the act of dying.

7

"It turns out that your last moments of life are busy. A lot of things, chemical things, have to happen before you can die. We're learning about that process, and how to stop it.

"What we've discovered is that if you stay in shock for very long, you're dead. Maybe you'll die in ten minutes or maybe you'll die next week, but you're dead. So if you're in shock we have to work fast. You've got, at most, sixty minutes. If I can get to you, and stop your bleeding, and restore your blood pressure, within an hour of your accident . . . then I can probably save you. I call that the golden hour."

Cowley climbs the steps to the first floor and pushes through two sets of doors into the outer admitting area. The smell of antiseptic is strong.

"They come up the elevator and through here," he says, reaching into a bin and withdrawing a long pink gown. He wraps the gown around his street clothes, puts a paper cap on his head and fastens a surgical mask over his mouth and nose. A meaty hand touches a pressure switch on the wall and a pair of massive oak doors swing wide, releasing compressed air.

"This is the overflow admitting area on your left," he says, jerking a thumb toward an open room. Inside, three steel surgical tables stand surrounded by sheet-draped instruments.

"We keep this whole area as clean as possible," Cowley says. "Sometimes there's no time to get into the operating room. We can crack a chest right here if we have to."

Farther down the hall, a small and highly-illuminated alcove opens to the left. Monitors, racks of intravenous fluids and cabinets of surgical supplies occupy every available space. Cowley stops.

"Sometimes we have three or four admissions at once and then this place is incredible. In a disaster, we can even do procedures outside in the hall, but mostly we use the primary admitting area here."

Inside the alcove, two nurses move quickly around a single surgical table, laying out sterile equipment and breaking open packages of catheters and hypodermic syringes. The younger of the two women, a twenty-three-year-old probationary trauma nurse, works from a printed checklist.

High on the far wall a bright green dot moves in a straight line across a television screen. A large, wire-reinforced window set into an adjacent wall looks out over a deserted operating theatre.

Outside the alcove there is a surgical deep sink, and Cowley leans against that. "This is where we stabilize the patient, keep him breathing, keep his heart going. Heartbeat and breathing. Those two things are critical."

Maryland's system for rescuing dying motorists is designed to attend to those primary imperatives, heartbeat and breathing, heartbeat and breathing, heartbeat and breathing. And if the style of medicine practiced in the trauma unit resembles that of an army field hospital, Cowley acknowledges the debt. Wars, for all their horrors, are meccas of learning for young surgeons and it was the army that first introduced him to traumatic shock.

Cowley was in medical school and his surgical residency during World War II, so he missed the battlefield experience. But, sent to Europe soon after the fighting stopped, he discovered that there is also abundant surgical opportunity in war's aftermath. Bombed-out buildings collapse. Old ordnance explodes. Bored with occupation duties, men fight among themselves.

And most of all in those days, the shell-damaged roads buzzed with badly-designed, top-heavy jeeps that mixed poorly with French wine. In 1946 Cowley worked under virtual wartime conditions in the operating rooms of an army field hospital in Mourmalon, France.

When the jeep casualties piled up and there were too few doctors and operating rooms, Cowley was forced to turn his back on the most severely injured patients. His limited time would be better spent saving men with lesser wounds. The strategy, designed to maximize the lifesaving ability of a field hospital, is called triage. It was as repugnant to Cowley as it was and is to other doctors but, as doctors always had, he bent to the realities of the moment.

Speed, under such circumstances, becomes a compulsion. The faster a military surgeon can operate, the fewer times he must turn his back. The young doctor from Utah, his Hippocratic oath fresh in his mind, arrived in the operating suites at seven in the morning. He usually stayed until nine or ten at night.

Soon he began to take pride in the quickness of his knife. His reputation grew and he became chief of surgery. Later, he was transferred to the Ninety-eighth General Hospital in Munich.

There the hospital commander occasionally rewarded his bright young chief of surgery by sending him to the famous Allgemeine Krankenhaus in Vienna. Some of the Continent's greatest old-school surgeons were still alive and operating there, and Cowley was spellbound by their skill. He'd never seen surgeons work so fast.

"These men . . . one swipe of the knife and the belly was open. Not like us, going through layers at a time and stopping the bleeding as we go. They'd slap on towels, do it barehanded.

"Quick as they'd get down to the guts they'd put on a pair of cotton gloves so that they could hold the bowel without slipping and sliding. They'd do their stuff, and they were finished. They were so good, and so clever, that what would take three hours in America would be over in forty minutes."

Cowley admired the old-fashioned skill, but he was impressed even more with the results. In Vienna, fewer patients died. Recovery was quicker. Cowley wondered . . . might it be the speed?

All his instincts said yes. As an army hospital surgeon he was fast because he had to be, and his patients seemed to do well despite the primitive conditions and equipment. When he returned to the United States to train as a heart surgeon, he capitalized on his ability to think and act quickly.

Those skills eventually allowed him to join the small number of surgeons who performed open-heart surgery even before the advent of the heart-lung machines. Cooling the patient beforehand to slow the metabolism, Cowley would cut into the heart, repair the drainage, close the incision and restart the heart in less time than it took the brain to suffocate.

Outside the heart surgery suites, Cowley the scientist blossomed. He became deeply involved in the race to build the heart-lung machine, invented a surgical clamp that bears his name and developed the prototype of the electronic pacemaker that was always kept with President Eisenhower.

"Heart surgery was the frontier then," Cowley remembers. "We were doing things nobody had ever thought could be done. We were incredibly careful, we worked as a team, and we did our job perfectly. We got the patient through the operation and into the recovery room."

Cowley pauses in his narrative and his voice grows softer. "And then, goddamnit, he would die. He would go into shock and die."

Other heart surgeons also lost patients to post-surgical shock, of course, but most of them did their best and went home to their families. Something in Cowley's strict Mormon programming wouldn't let him do that, wife or no wife, child or no child.

They were *his* patients and *his* responsibility, so he spent his evenings training nurses and his nights in the laboratory, hoping to tease the deadly secret out of the tissues of bled-out dogs. What was shock?

In those days not much was known about shock except that, in its classic form, it immediately followed the extreme loss of blood pressure caused by heavy bleeding. When Cowley operated on a heart the patient had no blood pressure at all for a few minutes but— and here was the difference—his patients didn't go into shock immediately. It came later, hours or days later, as infection set in and the patient lapsed into a deep coma.

Cowley sought answers in his dog lab. Carefully, using instruments to monitor the animals' vital signs, he drained their blood into sterile bottles. After a predetermined number of minutes, the blood was dripped back into the now-shocky animal. The data were carefully recorded.

Cowley's deepest scientific prejudice was that the clues he needed would emerge from the numbers. Sometimes the dogs died and sometimes they didn't. What was the difference? Cowley juggled the statistical data. Months passed, then more than a year.

When the pattern finally began to emerge, the heart surgeon spent even more time in the laboratory, often sleeping there at night. His wife and daughter saw him less and less.

Years later the Shocktrauma psychiatrist, Dr. Nathan Schnaper, would repeatedly urge Cowley to develop a personal life, to get out, to think about something else. Cowley would politely ignore the advice.

"He's gotta be here all the time," says Dr. Schnaper. "He's compulsive, that's all there is to it. Maybe someone he respected once called him stupid. I don't know. Whatever it was it made him insecure enough that he compensated by becoming a genius.

"You know," says the psychiatrist, sighing, "it's an argument for celibacy. A genius is like a priest. Cowley should never have married. When a guy dedicates himself to something the way he has, his family has got to suffer. It's infidelity of the worst kind. This place is his wife, his mistress, his baby ... it's the reason Nobel laureates often have screwed-up personal lives."

In the dog lab days Cowley and his wife began to drift irreconcilably apart, and eventually she moved back to Utah. Cowley had lost his family, but he found his numbers.

Today, his hair turning gray, the heart surgeon leans against the surgical sink outside Admitting Area One and remembers those numbers. The numbers that counted weren't the ones on the sophisticated instruments; they were the ones on the clock. Time was critical.

By taking a quart of blood from a laboratory dog, Cowley could make the animal lapse into shock. If he returned the blood quickly, the dog would be sick for several days, but in the end it would recover.

But if the animal remained in shock for more than an hour, the scenario changed. Return of the blood still revived the dog, but the rally was temporary. Some unknown and insidious process set in motion by the shock would proceed unseen and in seven days, or ten, the hidden changes would manifest themselves. The dog's biochemical machinery faltered, its temperature rose and bacteria swam in its blood. The canine heart pounded crazily, the fever rose still higher and the fangs snapped at nonexistent tormentors. Death came slowly, just as it did to Cowley's heart patients.

The numbers told Cowley that the heart surgery patient who died of secondary shock never had a chance, that his apparent good condition in the recovery room was a cruel hoax.

After all, the patient's circulatory system was in bad shape or he wouldn't need heart surgery in the first place. The body was in chronic shock. Added to that, the effect of the heart stoppage was sufficient to set in motion the subtle and mysterious process which, several days later, would cause death.

In other words, the longer a patient was in shock, the more likely he was to die. It was simple, and revolutionary.

"The system you see here is fast," Cowley says, folding his arms and settling back against the sink. "Not only that, it's very democratic. Sometimes it takes two or three hours for a patient's name to catch up with him. We're that fast. We don't care who he is. All we know when he comes in here is that he's hurt. If he got into our system, he's dying. We don't care whether or not he has a Blue Cross card. There isn't time.... "

"Dr. Cowley," a freckle-faced nurse interrupts. "Get out of the way, please."

Cowley stops in mid-sentence. He sighs. Shock-trauma nurses are special, and they have special privileges. That includes the right to bully the director.

So R Adams Cowley, M.D., heart surgeon, patron saint of dying motorists, the man the Secret Service would call if the President were injured, slinks out of the admitting area, abashed. He touches another wall switch and moves through the hissing doors. The operating room lounge and the coffee he smells are to his right.

Two surgeons, the admitting team leader and Cowley's chief neurosurgeon, are sitting on a counter beside the coffee pot, talking in low tones. They slide to their feet as Cowley enters.

"Howdy, Tex," the heart surgeon says to the team leader. "Got one on the way, I take it."

"Yes, sir," says Tex. "From the scene."

Cowley fills a Styrofoam cup with thick black coffee and the junior surgeons resume their conversation.

Cowley, coffee in hand, mask still on his face, wanders out into the hallway. "Time . . . " he muses, pulling aside the mask to sip at the coffee. "It's the little things that kill. They didn't mean anything at the time, but days later you see the patient start to die. You know you missed something and you'd like to go back and do it over, but you can't. It's too late. You can spend money, train doctors and nurses, develop drugs . . . but if you wait too long none of these things will help. Time is the one thing you can't buy."

A loudspeaker on the wall beeps twice. "THERE WILL BE AN ADMISSION IN TWO MINUTES," a voice says.

3

ON THE ROOF OF THE PARKING GARAGE THE MED-
ics run beneath the helicopter rotors, pulling the
stretcher. The stretcher glides feet-first into the rear
compartment of the ambulance and locks into place
with a sharp snap. Inside, the nurse kneels, releases the
safety straps across the patient's chest and throws aside
the gray military blanket. The ambulance attendant
slides in beside the nurse, the Bengali anesthesiologist
steps into the rear and the doors close, muffling the
noise of the jet engines. The ambulance rocks in the
downdraft as the helicopter lifts clear of the roof.
Shovel-nosed scissors cut away the boy's clothing.

The vehicle lurches as it descends the steep spiral
ramp, its red and white emergency lights playing across
the parked cars. Inside, the nurse grasps an overhead
railing with her left hand and surveys the boy's naked
body. Blood oozes from a deep cut over the right eye
and a plastic, inflatable splint covers the upper segment
of the right leg. A small amount of blood oozes from

the top of the cast. The nurse can only guess what lies beneath the bloodsoaked turban on the boy's head.

Her right hand goes automatically to the groin, pushing aside the adolescent testicles to probe for an artery. Her eyes lose their focus as her fingers search the flesh and finally feel the pulse, weak and rapid.

The nurse moves her hand to the belly, smearing blood across the icy white skin. As her hands explore the body further they discover tiny blisters of gas beneath the right armpit—air escaping from a punctured lung.

The Bengali anesthesiologist shines a penlight into the boy's eyes. Very slow, too slowly, the pupils contract. The brain, deprived of blood-carrying oxygen, is beginning to suffocate and the patient is dying. It is 7:26 P.M.

The ambulance driver touches a red button as he eases the vehicle out of the parking garage and into Redwood Street. The siren echoes in the tight canyon of hospital buildings and the emergency flashers sweep across red brick. It is only a matter of yards but the nurse can no longer find a pulse. She presses her stethoscope against the boy's chest. The anesthesiologist digs his fingers hard into the neck, seeking a carotid pulse. There is none. There is no heartbeat.

Ahead, at the dead end of the brick canyon, a huge trash dumpster stands beside a concrete loading dock. A black man in hip boots moves across the slippery concrete pier, sweeping away garbage with a stream of water from a high-pressure hose. A grapefruit rind from the cafeteria, caught by the force of the water, flies off the pier and rolls under the dumpster. The man turns off the nozzle as the ambulance comes to a stop and its doors explode open.

The nurse jumps on the stretcher as soon as the medics have it on the ground. Her knees straddle the boy's torso. Placing both hands over the sternum, she throws her weight repeatedly against the boy's chest. The attendants pull the stretcher and the anesthesiologist duckwalks beside the patient's head, feeding bottled oxygen into the damaged lungs.

A woman and a small boy flatten themselves against the wall as the trauma team travels the red line, the nurse riding the stretcher, heaving against the naked chest. An ambulance medic kicks aside the sign and the stretcher rolls into the waiting elevator. The doors close. The nurse's breathing is loud in the confined space. Each time she thrusts against the chest, the boy jerks. The doors open.

The nurse jumps clear as the stretcher rolls into the admitting area. "He arrested out back in the ambo," she says to the team leader, the surgeon Cowley had called Tex. "His pupils are slow, there's a right pneumothorax, and I think he's a belly."

The clock on the wall says 7:30.

4

THE COMMOTION IN THE ADMITTING AREA PENE-
trates into the operating corridor, but Cowley doesn't
seem to notice. He says all multiple trauma victims
deserve the level of care provided by the shocktrauma
unit, but they rarely get it.

"The God's truth is that most emergency rooms are
awful," he says. "I get into trouble every time I say
that and some miserable son of a bitch quotes me in
the newspaper, but it's true. Even today you live or die
depending on where you have your accident, because
in most places they take you to the nearest hospital."

Cowley's contempt for the slapdash methods of the
emergency room is deep and abiding. He trained, after
all, in the antiseptic efficiency of open-heart surgery.
The struggle with death, he knew from the beginning,
required precision medicine.

But in the late 1950s even precision medicine failed
the heart surgeon. The surgery was successful but the
patient died. It was a hospital joke. It happened all the
time.

Cowley wasn't the only heart surgeon to endure the frustration, but he was one of the few who thought the deaths were avoidable. His dog experiments had convinced him that if only he could understand the exact series of hidden events that led to secondary shock, he could intervene. But first he had to know a great deal more about dying, and the dog studies were not enough. Cowley needed to know about people.

Early in 1961 he opened a two-room hospital laboratory equipped with every sort of monitor a heart surgeon could procure. One of the two rooms was packed with equipment for chemical analysis. The second room contained a single bed, dwarfed by banks of electronic equipment. The laboratory's formal title was the Clinical Shock Trauma Unit, but its function was to monitor and study the act of death in humans.

In the death lab, doctors and nurses clustered around the single dying patient, recording every available vital sign and metabolic variable. They drew blood, analyzed urine and listened to the heart sounds as the patient slid deeper and deeper into shock. After each one died, Cowley's doctors began searching for another candidate.

"We were the black birds of the hospital, man," chuckles Dr. David Boyd, one of Cowley's star pupils. "Whenever we showed up on the wards the nurses would dive for their charts to see who was in shock. Whenever we were around somebody was dying."

When a prospective patient was located, his doctor was often very cooperative. Death with dignity had not yet become fashionable, and the family was usually begging the physician to do anything, anything at all. When

21

Cowley offered to take the patient, well, after all, the fourth floor laboratory was about as sophisticated a set-up as medicine had to offer.

Family members, when they visited the patient, were usually impressed by the blinking lights and the hovering doctors and nurses. A respirator, which then was still primarily an operating room device, was frequently in use. Nutrients and other vital metabolic chemicals dripped into the patient's body and plastic tubing dipped beneath his skin to monitor conditions in the circulatory system.

Once each hour the nurse drew a sample of blood, and a laboratory attendant next door spent what remained of the hour taking that blood sample apart, molecule by molecule. Cowley and his nurses received constantly updated bulletins on the fluctuations of most of the important metabolic chemicals. Hour by hour they knew the abundance of red blood cells, the availability of oxygen-carrying hemoglobin, the breakdown rate of the liver, the contents of the urine and the cellular balance between oxygen and waste carbon dioxide.

As Cowley bent over the graphs, charts and lists of numbers, he was intrigued by the fluctuations. They were oscillations, really. Back and forth, back and forth. As death approached even the blood pressure began to rise and fall, rise and fall. Protein levels, hormone levels, enzyme levels . . . oscillating. The metabolism seemed to be shaking itself apart, the fluctuations grew wilder and wilder until something went fatally wrong and the whole human colony of human cells got

22

so out of step that chaos ruled and the heart stopped and the patient died.

Other doctors had made all the measurements before, but they'd made them once a day, not hourly, never by the minute. The growing oscillations were never revealed. But now Cowley knew about them and, knowing about them, was duty bound to treat them. When the blood began to turn acid, buffers were injected immediately and that oscillation never got started. When the blood oxygen levels fell, the respirator was adjusted. And sometimes, in this fashion, the snowballing oscillations were prevented entirely and the patient recovered. From the beginning, half the people brought to the death lab to die, didn't. As they improved they were returned to their doctors who in turn sent them back to their grateful families.

Cowley was ecstatic. The snowball was in fact composed of snowflakes, of fluctuating blood pressures and wobbling sodium balances, of increasing acidity and tides of adrenaline. When those things could be corrected as they occurred, the snowball didn't develop.

The next question followed naturally. Cowley wondered what would happen if he could get the patients earlier, before the dying process got started. Not waiting for the symptoms of shock, he moved his sickest heart surgery patients directly from the operating room to the death lab. His heart surgery survival rate took a sharp curve upward.

Cowley's death lab procedure was occasionally interrupted by highway crash victims who were too shattered for the emergency room to handle but still too alive for the morgue. In the death lab, they frequently survived.

As the data accumulated, Cowley began to visualize shock as a logistics problem within the human colony of deftly orchestrated cells. The bottleneck seemed to involve oxygen and circulation and, in particular, the circulation through the microscopic capillaries that are the all-important back streets of the body. Heart surgeons have a word for it: perfusion.

The heart pumps the red, oxygen-carrying blood from the lungs and out into the body. Eventually forced into the capillaries, the red blood cells squeeze single file between the cells of the body.

As the blood moves through the capillaries, oxygen and nutrients diffuse outward to the surrounding tissue. By the same process, called osmosis, carbon dioxide and other waste products collect in the bloodstream. Eventually the blood pours out into the low-pressure veins for purification and transport back to the lungs, where the process begins once more.

If the circulation process is interrupted in any way or for any reason, from old age to decapitation, the cells immediately begin to suffocate. Oxygen can't be stored and brain cells, which are most vulnerable, die in six minutes. Kidney cells can hang on for an hour or more.

Most of Cowley's heart patients suffered from a chronic lack of perfusion, and while heart surgery and the death lab saved them for the moment, the surgeon knew they would soon be dead. At best they would survive a few weeks.

In this respect, the accident victims were different. Most of them were teenagers and young men in their

24

most productive years. They were healthy, except for their massive injuries, and when they lived they usually recovered completely. The benefit to the patient, as well as to society, was unmistakable.

One observation in particular gave Cowley pause. In the United States alone 50,000 people died on the highways each year—more than eight hundred in his own state of Maryland. If he had a big enough death lab, and could get them to it quickly enough, he could save at least half of them. Even by a heart surgeon's standards, that's a lot of lives.

People were dying, unnecessarily. Cowley knew his duty.

Now, a generation later, Cowley stands in the sterile corridor and stares with unfocused eyes at an operating room door. The memories are still bitter. He had really expected people to care about those 50,000 lives. Or if not people in general, at least Cowley's fellow doctors. But he found himself very much alone.

"No one had ever set up a real system to take care of accident victims," he says. "They'd scrape you off the highway, put you in a hearse and take you to the closest hospital.

"If you had multiple injuries, they wouldn't be ready for you. They wouldn't have the blood. Most accidents happen at night, when the labs are closed. Often the most senior person in the emergency room was a nurse, and she'd have to send somebody to find the doctor.

"Later the family would tell the physician that they knew he did all he could, and they were grateful. The doctor would honestly think he'd done all he could. The nurse would think she'd done all she could. Everyone would think that, but they were wrong. They could have recognized that they were in over their heads and sent the patient on to a better hospital."

Cowley shakes his head. "That's how it was then and that's how it still is, in a lot of places."

With his elbow, he nudges a wall switch and the big double doors swing open. As he steps into the admitting area, the freckled nurse rushes by with a syringe of blood in her hand. As her toe catches in a pile of wet clothing, she lurches sideways, off balance, falling. Holding his coffee cup, Cowley steadies her with his left hand.

Regaining control, the nurse winks at Cowley. He grins. When she is gone he picks up the clothing, carries it at arm's length to the side of the room and deposits it in a paper bag.

"In a small hospital, a lot of these people are dead on arrival. DOA is not a term we use here. There are no DOA's. There are only failures to resuscitate."

Pulling the paper cap from his head Cowley walks slowly out of the admitting area. His shoes go squish, squish, squish, leaving footprints of blood on the tile.

5

_____

THE YOUNG BOY LIES ON THE METAL TABLE IN THE
center of Admitting One, arms flung wide, naked except
for a covering of bloodsoaked bandages laid over the
bone that protrudes from his upper right leg. A hard
plastic fitting extends out of his cold, purple lips. Except
for the extended legs, the patient's entire body is
screened from view by the medical team.

Tex, the team leader, works above the right hip.
Frank, a senior Johns Hopkins surgical resident and the
team's second in command, stands by the opposite hip.
As they scrub the boy's groin with foaming brown antiseptic, bubbles collect in the thin pubic hair.

Returning from the laboratory, the freckled nurse
squeezes behind Tex and begins laying out surgical instruments on a tray. A senior medical student stands
on a stool by the left armpit, continuing the closed chest
massage.

"Freckles," says Tex, holding out his left hand.
Freckles lays a scalpel in it.

On each side of the boy's groin, beneath the tender

27

skin where lower belly meets upper leg, a branch of the big saphenous vein lies an inch beneath the surface. It is the avenue through which spent blood from the leg returns to the heart and lungs for recycling, and it often grows to the size of a soda straw—huge, for a shallow vein. Normally a third-year medical student can feel it with his fingers and, if need be, find it with a needle. But now, in shock, the collapsed vein is impossible to locate by touch.

The Texan's scalpel cuts deep. Dark, sluggish blood appears slowly at the wound, and is quickly sponged away as the honed steel slices again and again, digging, exploring toward the big vein. Across the table, the resident's knife parts the soft skin in the other groin.

The Texan's gloved fingers probe the pink wound, find the vein and pull it up like a large worm caught by the midsection. As the second hand of the clock on the wall sweeps slowly toward 7:34, he slips a hemostat under it to prevent it from slithering back into the groin.

Albert Einstein once explained relativity in terms of warm girls and hot stoves. A thirty-second kiss lasts but a fleeting instant, he said, while a half-minute on a hot stove is an eternity. For Einstein it was proximity to the speed of light that slowed time, but in the shock-trauma unit it is the nearness of death that stretches the seconds. That, and the adrenaline.

There are eight people on the admitting team: the Texan, the anesthesiologist, the surgical resident from the Hopkins, two medical students from the University of Maryland, two experienced Shocktrauma nurses and the nurse trainee. Each has a specific function. Each is absolutely alone.

Rapidly, they perform their familiar duties. Freckles's partner sticks electrocardiograph leads onto the boy's upper body, ducking in and around the medical student who pumps on the chest, sweat streaming from his face. Freckles tends the surgeons. The anesthesiologist attaches a black hose to the fitting in the boy's mouth. The second medical student cuts into the right forearm in search of a vein. The nurse trainee attempts to wrap a blood pressure cuff around the right bicep but she finds it difficult to work in the cramped space. It is precisely 7:34. With the tip of his scalpel, the Texan makes a small slit in the saphenous vein.

Beyond the boy's head, the anesthesiologist's brown hands touch the dials lightly, reach for a notebook. Pure oxygen, the gas of life, hisses through the plastic tubing and the boy's lungs expand under the broken ribs.

Bending over the extended right forearm, one of the residents digs in bloody muscle for another blood channel. In the meantime the Texan threads a large plastic tube into the saphenous vein and fastens it there with one quick suture. The tube, designed to force-feed infants, allows the maximum passage of fluid in the minimum time. As the team leader finishes the suture, Freckles turns a plastic knob and the tube fills with blood plasma. The clock continues to move, unwatched.

Crowded between the anesthesiologist and the medical student, the nurse trainee jostles the medical student's arm as she attempts to fasten the blood pressure cuff.

"Pay attention to what you're doing," he snaps.

A hurt look on her face, the trainee backs into the

respirator, earning a scowl from the anesthesiologist. Across the room, Freckles raises her face from a tray of scalpels and her eyes meet those of the trainee. Freckles's right eye winks.

As two bottles of plasma pour into the boy's body, the team leader steps back. A nurse places the defibrillator paddles into his hands. Instantly the team, including the man doing the closed chest heart massage, stands clear.

As the Texan presses the paddles against the boy's chest, Freckles whispers into the trainee's ear, "Take a deep breath. You get used to it. Honest."

"Now," says the Texan.

The unconscious body convulses as the current flows through it.

The ball point pen on the EKG machine swings from side to side, three sharp spikes, then another, two more in rapid succession, another, another, another, and finally a steady tic-tic-tic, much faster than the flow of seconds.

It is 7:38. The anesthesiologist makes a note in his book. The nurse trainee, stethoscope pressed against the inside of the boy's elbow, listens for the rattle of blood through an artery. Freckles lifts the bandage on the boy's right leg as the team leader watches. The sharp stub of living femur protrudes from a rip halfway between the knee and the hip. Blood clots jacket the exposed marrow.

The team leader stands above Freckles, his eyes moving from the bone to the leg and up the body. The two bottles of plasma are gone now, empty, replaced by bags of type O blood. There isn't time to do blood typing. Automatically, as his eyes move, the Texan's hands go up, wrap around the blood bags and squeeze hard, increasing the flow.

The team leader's mind moves through an inner library composed of facts and probabilities painfully accumulated during four years of pre-med at the University of Houston, four years of medical school at Baylor and a general surgical residency in Seattle where it rained every goddamned weekend for two years. His mind organizes itself around Cowley's checklist.

A thigh fracture, particularly when the bone protrudes, can bleed badly enough to empty the body of blood, stopping the heart. There was blood on the leg dressing but, the surgeon decides instantly, not enough of it to explain the cardiac arrest. His attention goes to the head of the table, where the anesthesiologist is stripping the turban of bandages off the boy's skull. An injury to the head can lower blood pressure too, and the scalp is rich in blood vessels. A scalp wound can bleed like almost no other, but the surgeon adds the blood on the leg bandage to the blood on the head wrapping and the total still doesn't explain the cardiac arrest.

His hands squeezing the blood bags, the surgeon's eyes go to the patient's lacerated chest. Broken ribs. Punctured lung. The aorta can tear loose in the impact of a high-speed collision, causing the patient to bleed to death inside the chest cavity. Quickly, automatically, the Texan reviews the procedures for slashing into the chest and pinching off a torn aorta with his fingers.

At the far end of the table, the stethoscope finally brings the sound of rushing blood into the nurse trainee's straining ears. She listens, intently, her eyes on the pressure cuff's dial.

"Blood pressure is 60," she calls out, triumphantly.

"Sixty?" the Texan repeats. "Shit. That's lower than a horny toad's hemorrhoids."

The anesthesiologist makes an entry in his notebook. It is 7:39 and thirty seconds.

Freckles winces. "You're a long way from Texas," she says. "Speak English. And move your hand."

The surgeon looks at his hand. It is still squeezing, but the blood bag is empty. He withdraws his fingers and Freckles hangs another bag of unmatched O.

An intercom on the wall beeps. "FIRST AREA," says a feminine voice.

"Yo," says the Texan.

"DO YOU HAVE A NAME ON YOUR PATIENT?"

The team leader looks at the nurse who rode over in the ambulance. "Negative," says the nurse. "We got him as a male Doe."

"Blood pressure is 70," says the trainee.

It is 7:41.

The team leader adds it up in his head. The boy has received three units of plasma, two of blood. Now four bags hang in the air, with lines running to the two saphenous veins in the groin and a vein in each arm.

The anesthesiologist announces that the head wound doesn't seem to penetrate the skull, then returns to his notebook and his dials. With carefully measured bursts of oxygen, the machine beside him fills the boy's lungs, then lets them partially—but never fully—collapse. The brand name on the machine is Engstrom. Engstrom is the Rolls-Royce of respirators.

The Hopkins resident, bending over the inside of the left elbow, has succeeded in threading a tiny sensor up into the antechamber of the boy's heart. The blood pressure readings come more regularly now. Seventy. Seventy-five. Eighty. Seventy. Seventy. Seventy-five.

Freckles hangs another bag of blood. The red liquid now runs through the heating coils before it spills into the body, but the first bags had gone directly from refrigerator to patient. The skin is cold to Tex's touch. Cold and white. Deep shock. The surgeon's mind works.

Chest . . . ?

. . . or belly?

"Upstairs," says the surgeon.

"THIS IS UPSTAIRS."

"See if the highway patrol knows who this boy is. I always like to know who I'm cuttin' on."

It is 7:44. The green dot hops rapidly across the television monitor.

6

THE SWEDISH-BUILT ENGSTROM RESPIRATOR THAT keeps the young patient's chest expanding is the most expensive production line model in the world. Shock-trauma has thirty of them and if the boy lives through the night their presence will keep him from dying tomorrow, or the day after, of shock lung. Shock lung was the terror of Vietnam and remains to this day one of the principal killers of accident victims. But nobody dies of shock lung in the trauma unit.

The reason is the Engstrom respirator, and Dr. T. Crawford McAslan, the punctilious, politely aloof Scotsman who solved the problem that had baffled the army's medical brass.

Shock lung was first noted in passing by surgeons who attended the wounded in World War I, but it wasn't a major problem because few badly-injured patients lived long enough to get it. Most of them bled to death, either in the mud or on the long, bumpy journey to the hospital. The big killer then was gangrene.

In the wars that followed, military doctors developed

a Mobile Army Surgical Hospital (MASH) system of trained medics, on-the-spot transfusions, quick evacuations and artificial respiration techniques that kept most injured soldiers alive long enough to get to the hospital. By Korea, military surgeons were beating back immediate shock and reviving the dead on a production-line basis, only to lose them later to kidney failure. Before the war ended, army doctors had developed the artificial kidney machine.

But even that victory was often academic in Vietnam. As the battles raged in the rice paddies and jungles, a wounded soldier who would have died quickly in earlier wars was drugged, transfused and flown directly to a field hospital to be revived, given more blood, stabilized and rushed directly into an operating room. A few hours later, his wounds sewed up, a dialysis machine standing by, the danger would seem well past. The following day his condition would be improved.

But then, perhaps forty-eight hours after the medic had run to his side, the soldier would become increasingly confused, then restless, then delirious. At the end he would choke and gasp, fighting for breath. A respirator would be attached to help him inhale, but the tactic rarely worked. Nine times out of ten the young man died.

The curious fact was that many of those who died of lung failure didn't have chest injuries. They had stepped on mines, taken machine gun bullets through the abdomen, or suffered concussion injuries to the liver or spleen. The only common denominator seemed to be shock. All the victims of lung failure had endured, at least briefly, the circulatory collapse of deep shock.

In the mid-1960s at University Hospital, when Cowley was the chief of heart surgery and McAslan worked for him, they had seen a similar and equally deadly sort of lung failure.

It happened to patients who had been attached to heart-lung machines for long periods of time, so they called it post-pump lung. Cowley and McAslan watched helplessly while their patients died as Vietnam soldiers would die, their lungs gradually stiffening and slowly filling with a liquid that finally welled up in the windpipe, producing the classic death rattle.

As McAslan thought more about post-pump lung, he began to develop a theory. It germinated in the anesthesiologist's disdain for cheap equipment. Simply put, he figured that fewer patients would die if the hospital would just give him better tools.

He was particularly incensed by the dime-store respirators the University of Maryland expected him to use. The machines were produced on an American assembly line, cost $500, and in McAslan's estimation did a poor job of keeping the lungs filled with air. He couldn't prove that the cheap respirators were killing patients, but his instincts told him they must be.

So he put together his argument and went to the hospital's budget-keepers and asked them to buy him the world's best respirator. An Engstrom was what he wanted. The budget executives patronized him, and McAslan came away bitter.

"At that time an Engstrom cost about $8,000. I said they wanted to treat people at Sears-Roebuck prices. I said if you want to treat them, you've got to pay the money, but they wouldn't buy me any Engstroms."

The budget people were indifferent to McAslan's judgement, but Cowley wasn't. Cowley listened and thought. He didn't laugh. He juggled the thoracic surgery division's budget instead, and the next year McAslan got his Engstrom.

"Only a man like Cowley would go for it," McAslan smiles. "This is the kind of thing he does. If something's crazy, he'll support it."

The gamble paid off. Cowley's heart patients continued to get post-pump lung, but when they were attached to Dr. McAslan's Engstrom respirator from the beginning, they didn't die.

McAslan didn't claim to know why that happened, but he could tell it was damned important. He mulled over the differences between the Engstrom and the standard, American-made respirator. The key, he decided, was that the cheap respirator allowed the patient's lungs to collapse completely between breaths. The Engstrom, by contrast, blew up the lungs and then just let them relax ... relax, never collapse entirely. There was always enough pressure in the Engstrom to keep the patient's lungs inflated a bit, which is why the company advertised it as a "positive pressure" device.

The conceptual jump was inevitable. If Engstroms could prevent post-pump lung, what about the soldiers in Vietnam? What about accident victims in the United States? Cowley and McAslan studied the problem and decided that post-pump lung and shock lung looked like different examples of the same dying process.

Then in 1968, at the height of the Vietnam war, the National Academy of Sciences summoned the nation's top shock experts to a discussion of shock lung and what to do about it. The most important thing that happened at that meeting was that McAslan, a relatively obscure scientist, came home convinced he could treat shock lung with Engstrom respirators.

Trusting the McAslan hunch, Cowley ordered Engstroms for the shocktrauma unit he was then fighting to build. McAslan packed his bags and departed to the Karolinska Institute in Stockholm, to study under Gunnar Engstrom himself.

When he returned to the University of Maryland a year later, the trauma unit was finished. "I told Dr. Cowley I was satisfied I could prevent respiratory failure," McAslan remembers. "And we started to treat patients."

The strategy was simple. Remembering that respirators didn't seem to help once the shock lung patient had begun to die, he hooked up the Engstrom at the first sign of respiratory distress. When in doubt, he treated first, on the most flimsy of symptoms. "I tried to compare it to putting up an umbrella before it rains," he said. "Then if it does rain, you don't get wet."

The argument didn't impress Dr. McAslan's colleagues, however. In treating the patients before full-blown shock lung developed, the anesthesiologist violated one of the most ancient and universally accepted principles of medicine.

To a medical pioneer, yesterday's dogma is a special threat. It's not the mysteries of nature that blind a scientist but his own unexamined prejudices, handed down to him from previous generations of scientists.

McAslan's own career, like Cowley's, was made particularly difficult by the principle that the doctor should approach any new patient in four steps. And those steps *must* be taken in order.

First, the physician must take a history, asking questions either of the patient himself or of a close relative. Is he sensitive to any drug? Has he had a heart attack previously? Is there cancer in the family? Is he a diabetic?

The second step is a physician's examination, which prompts more questions. Where did that scar come from? Does that hurt? Have you always had those bumps? Medical students learn to caress the patient's body, feeling for knowledge with their fingertips.

Today, the examination continues on a chemical and microscopic level. Blood is drawn for tests and scrapings are collected for the culture dishes.

History and examination complete, the physician ponders the information and, as the third step, makes a diagnosis. Only after those three steps are complete may treatment begin. Even in contemporary times, to vary from that order is to risk a lawsuit.

McAslan's sin was to begin respirator therapy before the symptoms of shock lung began to appear. In effect, he was treating a condition he couldn't prove even existed in a specific patient. His fellow scientists objected on ethical grounds. Unless the patient was obviously dying, the respirator should not be used. McAslan replied that even the Engstroms didn't help once shock lung had appeared. If saving lives meant he had to be unethical, then he would damned well be unethical.

Cowley backed McAslan without reservation. While the anesthesiologist was away in Stockholm, Cowley's new shocktrauma unit was, predictably, losing eight out of every ten patients who lapsed into shock lung. With McAslan on the job, the death rate fell quickly to four out of ten.

Despite his success in keeping shock lung from killing his patients, however, McAslan still didn't know what caused it . . . or how it might be prevented. In the end he developed and played out another theory.

He assumed that respiratory failure, like liver and kidney failure, was set in motion during the golden hour. It just didn't manifest itself for a day or two. On those grounds, he decided to open the umbrella sooner. Instead of waiting for the first hint of shock lung, McAslan wouldn't wait for any symptom at all. He'd just assume the patients were going to get it and hook them up to an Engstrom as part of the admitting area routine.

"I didn't know which ones were going to develop shock lung, so why not manage anyone with serious blunt injury to their body with respirators from the moment they come in here? If at the end of twenty-four hours we're wrong, and they haven't shown any sign of developing respiratory failure, we can always give them a good night's sleep and take them off. But if it does develop, we'll keep them on the machine, and at least we'll have them from the beginning."

By 1972 *Medical World News*, the *Time* magazine of human biology, reported that McAslan's controversial new therapy was getting generally bad reviews all over the country. The authorities quoted in the story lambasted the Cowley team for its radical ways and for the ethical heresy involved in treating before diagnosis.

On the other hand, the magazine conceded, "The

umbrella seems to work. While admissions have tripled over the past two years, the mortality rate has dropped dramatically."

By 1972 McAslan had reduced his shock lung death rate to just one in a hundred. Elsewhere in the United States doctors clung to dogma and inexpensive respirators while accident victims continued to suffocate at the same rate as before.

Two years later, the overall death rate in the unit was down to twenty percent. One in five died of infection, of heart failure secondary to shock, of brain damage or irreversible chemical chaos. But in 1974 not one of McAslan's patients succumbed to shock lung, and few have died of it since.

"Sure," admits McAslan, "we can be attacked on the grounds of unscrupulous management of patients who didn't need as much as we gave them. But the traditional methods have a high failure rate, and the price of missing a diagnosis is death."

The anesthesiologist folds his hands, neatly. "It is a very stiff penalty to pay."

7

IN ADMITTING ONE, THE BENGALI ANESTHESIOLO-
gist pulls back the boy's right eyelid and shines his penlight through the dilated pupil and onto the retina. The
sudden brilliance triggers optical circuits deep in the
brain and, if those circuits are responding properly, the
pupils will instantly contract to pinpoints of black.
When the brain is dead, the pupils don't respond at all.
This patient's pupils respond, but sluggishly. The brain
cells, exquisitely sensitive to a lack of oxygen or the
buildup of waste products in the blood, are suffocating.
The anesthesiologist reaches for his book.

The boy lies cold on the metal table, his skin glowing
white in the harsh lights, the smears of blood turning
brown. He hasn't moved. All around him cathode ray
tubes glow, dial hands jump, lights flash and blood
hangs from high racks, cascading downward inside plastic tubes.

"Blood pressure is 70," calls the nurse trainee. A
moment ago it was 75. Before that it was 60. Low,
dangerously low, and fluctuating. The Texan stands by

the boy's feet, his eyes closed tightly, fingertips of the now-contaminated gloves pressed to his forehead, lips pursed, thinking, thinking.

The admitting team has already pumped six pints of blood and plasma into the boy . . . this patient couldn't normally hold more than nine pints, yet his blood pressure doesn't rise. Clearly the blood is gushing out as fast as it's going in. Gushing out somewhere inside the body cavity.

The team leader thinks. Chest?

Or belly?

The time is 7:46.

Freckles reaches across the thigh and pulls back the foreskin on the boy's shriveled penis. She sponges brown antiseptic liquid over it and then, with gloved hands, forces a large plastic catheter into the tiny orifice. Slowly, quarter-inch by quarter-inch, the tube travels up the urethra toward the bladder. The far end of the catheter is attached to a clear plastic bag with graduated marks on it, and when the probe reaches its destination a few drops of yellow liquid move slowly through the tube and run down the side of the bag. A few drops, no more. The kidneys, like the brain, are in shock. Deep in the hollows of the boy's back two maroon-colored organs are dying, and the poisons they can no longer remove are circulating in the blood.

Chest or belly?

It is 7:47.

Chest?

The force of the crash broke ribs and ruptured a lung, which is why the tiny bubbles collect beneath the skin of his right side. They crackle like fresh Rice Krispies as the gloved hands of the Hopkins resident probes for the proper point. The resident's scalpel slices in beside the pectoralis major, a landmark muscle that stretches over the gap between the third and the fourth rib, just beneath the boy's armpit.

The resident forces the hard, hollow plastic trocar between the ribs, like a stake. The boy does not move. The resident asks for a suture.

"Blood pressure is 65," says the nurse trainee.

A few drops of blood move through the tube in the boy's chest. A few drops, but no more.

Belly, then.

Freckles and the team leader work swiftly, throwing sterile drapes over the patient's scrubbed midsection.

"Blood pressure is 70."

Tex pulls on clean gloves and calls for a scalpel. Freckles gives it to him. The patient is too cold, the blood pressure too low. If the heart stops again, it's over. The surgeon makes a vertical two-inch cut just below the navel. Blood flows out, thinner than before. It is losing its ability to clot.

"Blood pressure is 70."

It is 7:49.

"Upstairs," the Texan says. "Rustle me up one orthopod, and tell the attending not to take his pants off."

"ORTHOPEDICS AND THE ATTENDING SHOULD STAND BY. GOT IT," upstairs answers. "AND TELL ME, DOWNSTAIRS, DOES YOUR PATIENT HAVE A LARGE BLACK BIRTHMARK IN THE MIDDLE OF HIS BACK?"

"I been too busy trying to save him to take a look at his back," replies the team leader. "How come you ask?"

"I STILL CAN'T REACH THE FAMILY, BUT IF HE'S WHO THE NEIGHBORS THINK HE IS, HE'S A JEHOVAH'S WITNESS. YOU BETTER NOT GIVE HIM ANY BLOOD."

The nurse trainee, at the head of the table, freezes in the act of hanging another bag of unmatched O. She looks at the Texan.

The team leader's scalpel slides through the subcutaneous fat, just beneath the skin of the belly. The boy is trim and muscular, and the fat layer is thin, no more than an inch. The Texan does the job swiftly and carefully.

Underneath the subcutaneous fat there is a tough flesh called the anterior rectus sheath. That, too, parts under the knife. The blood begins to flow more freely and the surgeon pauses to burn the bleeding vessels shut with a cauterizing instrument. Then he picks up the scalpel again.

"DOWNSTAIRS?" says the loudspeaker. "DOWNSTAIRS?"

"Yo," says the surgeon, cutting.

"DID YOU HEAR WHAT I SAID?"

"Yo." Cutting.

"WELL, WHAT DOES 'YO' MEAN?"

"It means," says the surgeon, "that you don't have positive identification. And this boy here, he looks like a Baptist to me. Now why don't you go somewhere and read your Bible and if I get time later I'll flop him over and look for that birthmark."

The clock says 7:53. The blood pressure is 75.

The nurse trainee makes her decision and finishes hanging the bag of blood. Soon the red liquid flows into the patient.

"The blood pressure is 75."

The team leader, bending over the small slit in the abdomen, makes a final cut. The preperitoneal fat spreads away, revealing the tough, semitransparent peritoneum. The peritoneum is the inner lining of the belly cavity, and normally appears frosty white.

Now it is blue.

Adrenaline pumps in the surgeon's veins.

Belly.

"Upstairs!"

"THIS IS UPSTAIRS."

"Please ask the attending to come to the admitting area," the Texan says, in perfect English.

"YES, SIR," says upstairs.

The team leader makes a purse-string stitch around a dime-sized area in the center of the exposed peritoneum. Then, carefully, with the end of the scalpel, he makes a small nick in the center of the suture. A thin stream of blood spurts out of the incision and sprays across his sterile gloves. A tug on the purse-string suture ends the flow.

"Let's get moving," the Texan says, loudly.

"Blood pressure is 75," says the nurse trainee, then disconnects the monitor. The heartbeat on the screen jumps erratically as the leads are pulled free. There is a clatter of steel implement on steel tray and then the table, bottles hanging above, begins to roll out of the cubicle, toward the double doors to the operating rooms.

It is 7:59.

The admitting nurses don't follow the stretcher

46

through the doors. Operating room nurses, fresh, clean and prepared, take their places.

A yellow wall telephone rings. Freckles picks it up. As she listens she absently watches two cleanup men, dressed in sterile gowns, as they move into the admitting area with mops and antiseptic.

The nurse trainee slumps against the metal records table in the hall, her mask pulled down to her chin. Freckles hangs up the yellow telephone and touches her shoulder with the back of a hand.

"We've got a traffic accident from Western Maryland. Come along and we'll meet the helicopter. The fresh air will feel good."

8

FRECKLES RESTS THE BACK OF HER HEAD AGAINST
the cold metal wall of the elevator and closes her eyes.
From her right hand, cigarette smoke curls upward
and drifts near the ceiling. As the car drops the trainee huddles, silent and apart, beneath the unlit EMER-
GENCY HOLD sign. She stares at Freckles's worn white
shoes and her left hand absently fingers a tiny gold
anchor fastened in the lobe of her ear. Machinery
whines.

On the basement floor Freckles turns a key in the
elevator's electrical panel, locking the doors open. The
EMERGENCY HOLD fixture glows red. The trainee sets a
three-foot-high HOLD FOR ADMISSION sign in front of the
gaping entranceway.

Walking slowly, they follow the red line down the
long hallway. Freckles always walks slowly whenever
she can. Out of the corner of her eye she watches the
new nurse.

"It gets easier," she finally says. "You don't get used
to it but it gets easier."

The trainee, who is walking ahead, turns her head in an embarrassed glance backward. "Oh, it's not that bad," she says. A few paces later she explains that it wasn't the patient that bothered her. It was the rude doctor who bumped her and then gave her a hard time about it. Freckles frowns at the denial, but lets it pass.

"There's a lot of stress in this job," she continues, "but it's got its rewards, too. It keeps you sharp. It's educational. People who work here two or three years can go anywhere they want to."

Both women wear heavy jackets over the long pink gowns that protect their sterile scrub suits. As they near the garbage dock exit the chill increases, and they stop to fumble with zippers. Outside, the wind has died down, but the temperature has dropped and their breath emerges in white puffs. As they pass the towering, frost-covered tanks where the hospital's liquid oxygen is stored, Freckles slips on a patch of ice and avoids a fall only by grabbing the pole of a NO PARKING sign. Her cigarette disappears into a sewer grating and she curses, reaching automatically into her jacket pocket for another.

As they walk by the psychiatry building, Freckles says that the unit was supposed to have a ramp leading like a bridge from the top of the parking garage directly to the unit, but the University scuttled the idea, and Freckles resents it.

"In this neighborhood," she grumbles, "you can get raped just walking to your car."

The trainee asks why they didn't build the ramp. Freckles walks in silence, attempting to find a match that will stay lit. She doesn't know why. It has something to do with some bureaucratic feud that goes way back, before her time.

"I don't know that much of the background. You'll hear it all in the gossip mill, if you want to. Me, I take care of my patients and the hell with all the rest.

"But stick around and you'll see what I mean. I can remember when we had critical patients out in the hallways, and it wasn't like there were no beds. University Hospital had beds, just a few feet away, but they wouldn't let us use them. Lord knows why. Territory, I think. They're like a bunch of male baboons, all thumping their chests. Where do you park?"

The trainee says she has a permit for the Fremont Avenue lot and Freckles whistles, rolling her eyes. She tells the trainee to be sure and take a campus cop with her when she walks to her car after the shift change. Freckles points to a set of double doors that lead into a building across the street.

"They'll say they're busy, but they're not that busy. The best way is to walk over there, through those doors, and the desk sergeant is at the top of the steps. Just stand there and insist. They're supposed to do it, and they know it. A nurse from obstetrics got her purse grabbed the other day, credit cards and all. The son of a bitch even broke her arm."

The campus police, alerted by Systems Communication that a trauma patient is on the way, have unlocked the side door to the parking garage. Inside, both elevators are on the fourth floor. They wait. It's damp inside the concrete garage, which makes it seem even colder than outside. The trainee stamps her feet.

"You ought to know," Freckles says, "that the trauma unit is a separate institute, which is one reason you'll find it a lot different from where you were before . . . Norfolk, right? . . . wherever. This place will scramble your brains, but it's nice not having to do all the dirty work."

Freckles squints at the elevator panel. The cars are still on four. She taps her foot, and they wait. The noise of a jet engine carries far in the winter air, and there is still no sound.

"The big thing you've got to watch is getting too tight with the patients. It's easy to do here. The situation is more . . . intimate. They tend to be more your own age and some of them are a lot like you. It's easy to let it hurt you every time they hurt. You forget that if they don't die they get well and go home, and either way they quit hurting. You stay right here."

The elevators stay on four.

"Sometimes, though, the patients come back and see you later, and that's nice. This goddamned thing isn't working again. We're gonna have to use the stairs."

The elevators malfunction frequently, occasionally trapping some luckless nurse inside. On the other hand, it is eight flights of stairs to the helipad and the nurses uniformly hate the climb.

The first time Freckles walked up these stairs was three years ago, when she was the trainee spending a night with the admitting team. Orientation. Or baptism. That night the pregnant woman in the helo wasn't hurt badly but the medic thought she might be . . . there was a lot of blood . . . and the accident happened on the way to the hospital. Her daughter was born in the ambulance

51

on the roof of the Redwood Street parking garage.

Everyone at the trauma unit remembers his first admission vividly.

In Freckles's case, the patient came back recently, on her daughter's third birthday. She brought a homemade orange cake and cut it in the nurses' lounge, around the corner from the critical care recovery unit, while the nurses played with the toddler. Afterward, Freckles went into a restroom and cried, then washed her face in cold water until the redness disappeared from her eyes.

Freckles doesn't tell this story to the trainee, however. The stairs are too steep and her breath comes too hard. On the fourth floor landing she reaches for another cigarette, then draws her hand back quickly. It is a hard climb, and at the top of the stairs Freckles leans, panting, against the metal railing.

They await the helicopter in an ambulance parked on the far side of the roof, lights blinking. Freckles sits by the back door, but the trainee moves toward the front when the senior nurse lights another cigarette. The driver asks what's coming.

"It's supposed to be a head case, but I wouldn't bet on it," says Freckles, through a cloud of smoke.

"You never know until you evaluate them," she continues, talking now to the trainee. "The other day they brought in a guy . . . young man, too . . . who was a high cord. Somehow SYSCOM understood the patient was in full arrest. SYSCOM told the admitting people that and the admitting nurse had a lot of trouble getting through to them over the ambulance radio that he wasn't. She had a vision of somebody trying to do closed-chest heart massage on this poor man with a broken neck. When there's a lot going on, messages get confused."

"But I guess you like it," the trainee says. "You sound like you do."

"Well . . . " says Freckles, dodging. "One thing I can say for the place is that the nurses have clout. I can go directly to the director of nursing any time I want to and I don't think she takes orders from anybody. For that matter, Dr. Cowley comes around often enough that you can talk to him directly. Forget about going through channels, but if you can catch him in the area, he'll listen. It makes the administrators furious, but he'll listen. And the administrators can't do anything to you. Nurses here don't get hassled and they don't empty bedpans, so. . . . "

The ambulance driver points his finger toward the windshield, calling attention to the landing light that burns bright in the night sky. As Freckles steps out of the ambulance she flips her cigarette away and it arcs through the cold air, spinning, spewing sparks as it disappears over the side of the roof.

"Watch for the tail rotor," she shouts to the trainee. "Don't go anywhere near that tail." The trainee nods.

The yellow and white aircraft settles in slowly, rocking, the downblast sending tiny fragments of decaying concrete pelting against the side of the ambulance. The nurses hold their gauze caps in place with their right hands, waiting for the skids to grind against the pad.

The noise level plummets as the pilot cuts the jet engine to idle.

"Bend over," Freckles shouts, pushing down hard on the trainee's shoulder. They run low, beneath the whistling blades.

9

TEX HOLDS THE SCALPEL LIKE A DAGGER. A THIN layer of cream-colored fat appears as the knife slits the belly from breastbone downward, until the incision joins the smaller cut made for the belly tap.

"Blood pressure is 80. It's rising," the anesthesiologist announces.

If the pressure were higher, blood would spurt from the severed arteries. Instead, it oozes. That speeds the way. Tex cuts deeper, leaving the surgical resident to find and clamp the vessels with hemostats.

The scrub nurse, standing above Tex and to his left, passes the hemostats across the patient. Each hemostat makes a sharp snap as it bites into the raw end of an artery. Above her mask, the nurse's large, dark eyes are accentuated by artificial lashes.

"Jehovah will get you guys for this," she says.

Tex doesn't slow his cutting. "Aw, anybody can tell this boy's a Baptist. Look at him. It's obvious."

"Pressure is 85," the anesthesiologist intones. The clock reads 8:08.

Tex prides himself on being a fast surgeon under normal circumstances, and tonight there is a reason to hurry. His scalpel parts the tough membrane that lines the abdomen and blood cascades out, soaking the sterile drapes and running in rivulets onto Tex's paper operating room booties.

"Pressure is falling," the anesthesiologist barks. "75."

"Tamponade," Tex says.

He was afraid of that. The boy's pressure had begun to rise and he had wondered why. Now he knows. Tamponade. Counter-pressure. Torn arteries pumped blood into the belly cavity and at first the pressure fell. Then the admitting team pumped blood into the boy, and the belly got fuller. Finally, when the cavity was engorged with blood, the backpressure damped the bleeding. Now that the pressure has been relieved, the bleeding will resume full force.

The situation has simplified, now, to an outright race between death and the surgeon. The battleground is the belly, but the organ at stake is the head, where the patient's intelligence and personality are chemically engraved in the brain. The vascular tree is profoundly injured and Tex has only minutes to find that injury and repair it.

The vascular tree is one of the body's strangest organs, a hydraulic rapid-transit system designed to move vital chemicals and to collect waste from each individual cell of the body. The vascular tree's principal pump is the heart, which keeps the arteries full, but the muscular arteries themselves contract and relax rhythmically as they move the blood along. Branching and narrowing as they lead away from the heart, the arteries eventually force their pressurized blood out into the tissue itself. The plasma of the blood washes through the tiny microscopic capillaries that interlace the living cells.

As it flows, the plasma carries with it all the dissolved salts, hormones, nutrients and other necessities of cellular life. This soup is also thick with the various denizens of the bloodstream, including the immune system's bacteria-eating phagocyte and the critical red blood cell.

This red blood cell, and its travels through the body, is the kernel of Tex's surgical problem. The cell is red because it contains a molecule called hemoglobin, a finicky traveler that likes company. As the red blood cell passes through the lungs, the hemoglobin molecule grabs an oxygen molecule to take along. When it passes through the capillaries, the cells of the tissue snatch the oxygen away and offer, as a substitute, a molecule of waste carbon dioxide. Preferring oxygen, the hemoglobin trades in the carbon dioxide molecule during its next trip through the lungs.

But the passage of blood through the capillaries is powered totally by the arterial blood pressures. If those pressures fall, the oxygen-carrying red blood cells cease to squeeze between the tissue cells. Almost instantly, the cells begin to suffocate.

Most of the individual cells can make do temporarily with stored food and they can hold steady, for a while, without the hormones and other chemical messengers that travel in the bloodstream. But the laws of biochemistry conspire against the storage of oxygen, and the business of the hemoglobin molecule is consequently the weakest link in the metabolic process.

The cells suffocate at a variety of rates, some of them surviving for hours and even days. But the sensitive gray brain cells called neurons are the first to die.

Tex moves fast. First, he needs to see what he's doing, and that means getting the blood out of the abdomen. Pieces of absorbent cloth the size of hand towels disappear into the body cavity and are withdrawn sopping. A suction device slurps ineffectively.

"Pressure is 80," the anesthesiologist says. A blood-soaked cloth makes a wet sound as it slithers to the floor. The circulating nurse retrieves it and lays it on a table with the other used sponges, to be counted at her first opportunity.

His field now relatively clear of blood, Tex goes for the most common and obvious source of massive internal hemorrhage, the spleen. Scientists have written treatises on the subtle and problematic functions of the plum-colored little organ, but those expositions are of no value to Tex. He knows it ruptures easily, bleeds profusely and is entirely unnecessary to the patient.

Tex's gloved hands move almost instinctively to the upper left portion of the abdomen. Gently lifting it, he examines the large vessels by which it hangs. No tears. He rubs his thumb over the organ, wiping away the blood. Nothing. He slips a piece of clean sterile fabric behind it and returns it to its normal position. Later he will check the fabric for fresh blood.

"Pressure is 85."

With new blood pouring into the boy's veins, the pressure holds . . . but not high enough. In someone so

58

severely injured, a proper blood pressure would be higher than normal, perhaps 150. At 85, the blood moves sluggishly through the capillaries.

It is 8:35.

"This boy's getting awful cold," Tex observes. The chill is a real worry. The diminished blood flow in shock causes a temperature drop in its own right, and with the belly now open what warmth there is escapes into the operating room. The metabolic processes are less efficient at low temperatures, and a cool heart tires quickly. On the surgeon's command, the circulating nurse goes to fetch warm salt water.

"Pressure is 80."

After the spleen, the second most common source of profuse bleeding in the abdomen is the liver. Only the bottom of the liver is visible through Tex's incision, so he runs his hands inside the boy's body, under the diaphragm, and explores that organ by feel.

Tex closes his eyes as he probes along the tough capsule that encases the mushy liver tissue. The left lobe is the easiest to reach, and the capsule feels smooth and unbroken. But when the hand reaches behind the other lobe, the surgeon's eyes open.

"I think I found it," he announces. "It feels like goddamned watermelon pulp."

"Pressure is 90," the anesthesiologist says, writing in his notebook that a nurse is hanging still another pint of blood. By now, none of the blood in the boy's body is his own and the laboratory sends the anesthesiologist a running report on the status of what he has. The low hemoglobin count tells the Bengali that the stored blood is no longer as efficient an oxygen-carrier as it once was, and he adjusts the oxygen flow to the patient's lungs accordingly.

"Pressure is 95," he announces, glancing at a gauge.

Tex has both hands inside the body cavity, now, pressing the bleeding liver between his palms. It takes strength, but it's working. The pressure rises slowly but perceptibly.

"Hit that intercom, would you?" Tex asks the circulating nurse. When she complies he shouts, "Upstairs?"

"YES SIR," says a voice.

"Upstairs, where the hell is the attending? I thought he was on his way down here."

"I THINK HE'S WITH THE FAMILY," the voice says.

"Oh," says the surgeon, thinking. "Is he a Baptist?"

"I DON'T KNOW. DO YOU WANT ME TO BEEP THE ATTENDING?"

"Naw," says Tex, "leave him alone. But if you hear from him tell him I could sure use some help here."

"Pressure is 95." It is 8:44.

As Tex continues to put pressure on the liver, the surgical resident adjusts the big overhead lights in a futile attempt to get a view of the damage. As he does so Tex asks the anesthesiologist if the blood studies are back and the Bengali responds with a list of numbers that make Tex hiss through his teeth and frown. The blood clots by means of a special protein, fibrinogen, along with a worker cell called a platelet that obstructs the flow of blood with its own body. Tex does a calculation in his head and then orders the administration of enough of those two components to make the patient's blood coagulate faster.

Once again the anesthesiologist touches the dials on the Engstrom respirator, adjusting the mixture of oxygen, nitrous oxide and sterile air. Flickering, changing numbers flash on the seven-foot bank of electronic instruments beside him. He moves rapidly from small chore to small chore, making adjustments, recording numbers and checking flows. Anesthesiology is a profession described as hours of tedium punctuated by moments of sheer terror. In a crisis, the anesthesiologist is on the spot. Death is a chemical phenomenon to be avoided by chemical means and, if necessary, reversed by chemical therapies. And the anesthesiologist is the keeper of the chemicals.

Beside him a bright green dot bounces regularly across a monitor screen, leaving behind a luminescent tracing of the boy's heartbeat. At a glance the anesthesiologist can diagnose a developing chemical problem by the shape of the line.

The pressure sensors implanted earlier in the boy's veins now give the anesthesiologist pressure readings from both sides of the heart and from a peripheral artery in the right arm. Using pressure readings from those three locations, the Bengali can deduce the hydraulic condition of the entire vascular tree and can even compute the rate of perfusion—how rapidly the red blood cells are moving through the capillaries.

Every time the heart beats, the green dot bounces on the screen and the dials connected to the three blood pressure sensors bounce in rhythm. With each jump there is a small, audible beep.

The anesthesiologist is keenly attuned to the rhythm of the beep. If it falters, he is the one who must inject the life-saving drugs through the small sensor tube that enters the left arm, travels upward through a vein and now undulates in the current at the antechamber of the heart.

The Bengali turns suddenly toward the instruments, head cocked. Did the heart rate slow? The numbers on the instruments confirm his senses, but tell him the change was small.

The beep of the monitor dominates the operating room. While Tex bends over the exposed entrails and squeezes the liver between his flattened palms, the surgical resident cauterizes all the little arteries that didn't bleed before because the blood pressure was too low. Tex's tactic is working; the pressure is rising steadily and the bleeding from the surgical wound increases. Each time the electric tweezers make contact there is a small *bzzt*. The smell of burnt flesh hangs in the room.

"How long was he in arrest?" the scrub nurse asks.

"It was in the ambulance, I don't know," Tex answers. "But he started up for us real quick in the admitting area." He is in an awkward position, bending over the patient, and he tries to find a more comfortable posture. He fails, but the flow of blood seems to be abating.

"Pressure is 95," the anesthesiologist says.

While Tex continues to press off the flow of blood, the surgical resident pours warm sterile water in the body cavity. Tex feels the heat move around his hands. He waits. The flesh is cold, too cold, and the heart is slow, too slow. Tex, too, listens to the beeps. If it happens, he will have to slash through the chest wall and reach inside, wrap his hand around the muscle and squeeze, and squeeze, and hope.

"Is the defibrillator handy?" he asks the scrub nurse.

Automatically the nurse's hand goes out and touches the gauze-covered sterile paddles. "Right here," she assures him.

Through the heavy operating room window Tex can see the gray-haired attending surgeon standing at the surgical deep sink, lathering his hands and scrubbing with scouring pads. Tex watches him rinse them off and, holding his arms at chest level, back through the operating room door. The circulating nurse wraps a sterile paper gown around him and extends a pair of open rubber gloves.

"I talked to the family," the surgeon says to Tex, from across the room.

"Oboy," Tex mutters to the cover. "I can't wait." Then, to the senior surgeon, "Yeah?"

"They gave blanket consent. Anything he needs. I got it in writing."

Smile wrinkles appear above Tex's surgical mask. One blood-spattered foot reaches out and kicks a leg of the scrub nurse's stool.

"See there," he whispers to her. "I told you he was a Baptist."

10

CHRIS? CHRISTINE? CHRISTINE! CHRIS, CAN YOU HEAR
me? Wiggle your toes, Chris! Chris! Wiggle your toes
now. . . .

With his left thumb the neurosurgeon pulls up first
one eyelid and then the other, directing the beam of
his penlight against the retina. The sudden brilliance
sends urgent impulses flashing from the retina to the
optical centers of the brain and the brain, if healthy,
should respond instantly with orders for the pupils. Exposed to the same bright light the neurosurgeon's own
pupils would shrink quickly to the size of pinheads.
Christine's pupils, however, respond sluggishly. The
right one is a little faster than the left one.

Christine lies flaccid and unresponsive on a metal
table just inside the door to the overflow admitting area,
and the nurse trainee stands near her feet, mesmerized.
As an intensive care nurse in Norfolk, she treated old
people with wrinkled faces and gravelly voices, with
failing hearts and cancerous bowels. Old people are
expected to be sick. Christine is not old.

The suntanned form on the table is that of a young woman, fit and well-formed. It would be attractive in an evening gown and in tennis shorts it would turn heads. Now it's naked and there is a small black mole visible on the right hip, a flaw that lies well within the narrow white triangular shadow obviously cast by a bikini bottom. The strong brown legs attach to the white pelvis and beyond that there is a brown belly followed by rising white breasts with erect pink nipples. From overhead, plastic tubes drape downward.

Christine! Christine! the neurosurgeon continues to shout, bending low over the delicate curvature of his patient's ear. From within that ear a small stream of blood flows downward and collects in the pillow of long, straw-blonde hair.

The nurse trainee takes a step backward as the neurosurgeon moves to the foot of the table, fishing a metal-handled, rubber-tipped reflex hammer from beneath his sterile pink gown. His eyes watching Christine's face, he presses the metallic end of the hammer hard against the right heel and draws it upward, toward the toes. The scraping is forceful enough to leave a long white mark. Christine doesn't twitch. The neurosurgeon repeats the procedure on the other foot, again without reaction.

The nurses and back-up team admitting doctors who met Christine's stretcher are working steadily around her now, but there is no urgency in their movements. They have already threaded the sensor into the superior vena cava, the entranceway to the heart, and the central venous pressure is displayed on an overhead dial. The heartbeat across the screen is strong and steady, though somewhat slow, and her blood pressure is a normal 120 and stable. She was breathing in the helicopter but the breaths were shallow, and now the anesthesiologist tends the Engstrom respirator that breathes for her. All signs are normal, except the most important one.

Again the neurosurgeon shines the light in Christine's eyes, frowns and walks away.

There are still two empty beds in the overflow admitting area and the neurosurgeon walks to the most distant of these, stops, and begins reading the label on a hanging plasma bottle. Absently, he strokes his beard. Then he returns to the table.

Christine, he yells into the bleeding ear. *Chris! Chris?* As he yells, his right hand catches a pink nipple between thumb and forefinger. He squeezes and twists.

Christine doesn't move but the nurse trainee, at the foot of the table, turns away so quickly that she almost bumps into Freckles. "Come on," the senior nurse says. "Help me with the Foley catheter."

The black-striped autoclave tape pops audibly as Freckles rips open the cloth-wrapped package. As she adjusts the rubber gloves on her hands, the trainee empties a bottle of brown antiseptic into a sterile steel bowl. Freckles catches a cotton ball between the tips of her tweezers and swishes the ball in the liquid. The nurse trainee reaches for a vacuum-formed plastic package.

"That's a beautiful tan," the trainee says, her eyes on the patient's torso. "And I don't think it's a sun lamp, do you?"

The team leader looks up from the far end of the

table. "Speaking of suntans," he says to Freckles, "did you know Lisa was going to the Bahamas?"

With her left hand Freckles delicately spreads the patient's labia, revealing the small pink clitoris and, a quarter-inch below, the puckered opening of the urethra. Using a fresh cotton ball for each stroke, she deftly sterilizes first the labia, then the area between clitoris and vagina.

"She's going to Florida," Freckles replies, her voice muffled by the surgical mask. "Starting tomorrow I'm going back upstairs for two weeks to fill in. It's Florida, though. Who told you she was going to the Bahamas?"

The trainee pulls open the Foley package and Freckles, still holding the labia apart with her left hand, reaches her right into the sterile interior of the package and withdraws a long, pink tube. She dips the tube into a container of lubricant and then presses it against the opening of the urethra. The tube travels inward, gently, two, then three inches. Suddenly, the tube fills with bright yellow liquid.

"Well, she's going to the Bahamas now," the team leader says. "The way I get it, her husband knows some guy who's an executive, and he's flying down there tomorrow morning, early. Like 6 A.M. early. He's a troubleshooter or something, but anyway he offered to take Lisa and her husband along for nothing if they could get ready that soon. Lisa's been in a panic all night, trying to get someone to come in early. Her husband's packing. I wish it were me. I wish."

Christine's urine flows down the tube and gushes into the collecting bag at the foot of the table. The kidneys were never seriously deprived of oxygen, and they are functioning normally.

Freckles looks wide-eyed at the team leader. "Her husband's packing? Her husband's packing?" she asks incredulously. "Jesus."

Christine, can you hear me? the neurosurgeon shouts. Again his penlight tests each pupil. There is no change. *Hey, Christine! Chris!*

The X-ray technician appears in the door, her big machine parked out in the hallway. "You ready for me?" she asks, brightly.

As the technician drives the machine into the room and positions it alongside the patient, the team leader and the neurosurgeon drift away, talking in low tones. Freckles and the trainee stay behind to help the technician tape a plate on the far side of the patient's neck. The cervical spine is always checked first, since improperly moving a patient with a broken neck can be fatal. The two nurses put on heavy lead aprons as the X-ray technician focuses the machine.

"Have you heard about Lisa?" Freckles asks.

"You mean the Bahama boondoggle? Yeah. I wish I had her luck. The last time I went anywhere was two years ago, and that was to Pennsylvania. SHOOTING," she shouts.

The rest of the admitting crew jumps behind lead-reinforced partitions. The X-ray machine whines loudly and clicks twice.

"I mean about her husband," Freckles says. "They've gotta go at 6 A.M. and she's upstairs now. So her husband's going to pack."

"Poor Lisa," the tech says. "My husband packed for

us once. Once. Ever try to spend a week camping with no tampons?"

"That's what I mean," Freckles says.

The X-ray technician takes the exposed plate and leaves. The trainee touches the patient's shoulder, then leans over her ear. "Chris? Chris?" she says, softly, into the bloody ear. There is no response.

"She's so young," the trainee says.

Freckles, lost in thought, doesn't answer. Undaunted, the trainee plunges on. "She's nineteen. I've got a sister exactly her age," she says. "I mean that could be her right here. Has anybody at the unit had a relative come in here?"

"A few," Freckles answers distractedly, "We're all susceptible. It's a young person's disease."

In a few minutes the technician returns with the developed negative and clips it to the light board with a professional snap of photographic plastic. The neurosurgeon counts the vertebrae images, one, two, three, four, five, six, seven, touching each image with his index finger. The one you don't see is the one that's broken. They are all there. Intact.

The neurosurgeon returns to the bedside, once more shining his light into the eyes. They are still slow, maybe a little slower. The left eye is still slower than the right. *Chris? Christine? Christine! Wiggle your toes for me, Christine. Squeeze my hand. Christine? Can you hear me?*

The girl lies motionless.

Again the neurosurgeon runs his long fingers through the blonde hair, feeling for damage to the brain's bony case. The left eye is connected to the right hemisphere of the brain, so the damage must be on the right side of the brain. The neurosurgeon can find no sign of trauma on the right side of the skull, but on the left side there is a hard knot. Christine has a *contra coup* injury. *Contra coup* means "opposite the blow."

Surgeons who specialize in trauma talk about two collisions. The first is the impact of automobile against bridge abutment. The car stops but the unbelted passenger doesn't and the second collision occurs when the passenger strikes the inside of the car.

Dermot P. Byrnes, one of the trauma unit's pioneering neurosurgeons, talks about still a third collision: the brain against the inside of the skull.

"We deal mostly with deceleration injuries, with the shearing, the stressing and the actual tearing that goes on with it. The third collision occurs when your head hits the dashboard and your brain squashes up inside your head. It ruptures vessels and causes clots, even without much skull injury.

"This process happens in milliseconds. You get a high pressure area at the point of impact and a low-pressure area on the other side." On the colliding side you get bruising, which is not good, and on the opposite side the fabric of the brain stretches and tears . . . which is even worse. Such a patient's eyes, as do Christine's, contract at lopsided rates.

Christine! Christine! Christine!

The bloodflow from the ear has slowed, leaving a drying brown channel.

With Freckles assisting and the trainee working nearby, the team leader swabs antiseptic solution over the girl's belly, turning the flesh yellow-brown. The protocol continues. Belly tap. The trainee pauses to watch, frowning.

"Hey," she finally says as Freckles places a sterile drape over the lower body. "You really going to do that? That's a terrible thing to have show above a bikini."

The team leader looks at Freckles, eyebrows raised. "How else am I going to know?" he says to the trainee. Freckles drops a hemostat, interrupting the conversation. She asks the trainee to get her another belly pack.

The team leader slices into the abdomen and, by the time the trainee returns, reaches the tough, white peritoneum. Once, before the age of antibiotics, it took a brave surgeon to cut beyond this barrier. Now the team leader matter-of-factly nicks it, inserts a long piece of tubing into the body cavity, and stitches it in place. A bottle of sterile salt solution runs into the belly from a hanging bottle. When the water is all inside, the bottle will go on the floor and the fluid will run back out. If the fluid is pink, there's bleeding inside.

"Her husband's packing," Freckles says to no one in particular. "Her husband. God. Can you imagine?"

Chris! Squeeze my hand. Chris! Can you hear me?

Now the neurosurgeon and the X-ray technician take over. Freckles assists while they put an X-ray plate under her head and tape her to it. The power head of the X-ray machine is placed above the bridge of her nose. Working from a pre-packaged assembly of equipment, the neurosurgeon fills a fat syringe with dye. The long needle glints in the harsh light as the man lays it against the tanned throat, over the left carotid. The left

71

carotid conducts the principal river of blood to the right brain.

The skin dimples as the neurosurgeon slides the needle into the flesh. He presses hard on the plunger and the dye races into the artery. "Shoot," he commands.

"SHOOTING!" the X-ray technician yells. Her machine goes *bzzt* and *click-click*.

Behind the partition, Freckles and the trainee wait for the shooting to stop. From where they stand they can see the empty saline bottle that, drained, has been transferred to the floor. Slowly, the solution flows back into the bottle. It is not bloody.

"That's just great," the trainee says. "A scar for nothing."

Freckles ignores her.

"I have a sister that age. She's blonde too, and she's a freshman at Hood College...."

"Look," Freckles interrupts. "I really don't want to hear about your sister right now." She turns and walks toward the light board, where the X-ray technician has just hung the angiogram results.

The dye-filled carotid artery is sharply outlined along the length of the neck, but where the vessel dips beneath the skull and into the brain, the flow is almost entirely pinched off. Only a few fuzzy branches snake through the brain tissue for short distances before they turn indistinct and finally disappear.

Freckles had seen many angiograms like that, and she has never seen such a patient survive. Freckles no longer believes in miracles.

She walks back into the overflow admitting area,

where the anesthesiologist, alone, tends the patient. Freckles bends over the girl's right eyelid and exposes the retina to the harsh overhead light. Slowly, very slowly, the pupil attempts to respond.

"Upstairs?" Freckles says.

The intercom clicks. "YES?" says a female voice.

"Have Lisa call me down here."

"OKAY," the voice acknowledges, and clicks off.

"I just can't stand it," Freckles says, to herself.

11

THE SENIOR SURGEON MOVES ACROSS THE OPER-
ating room, threading his way between people and machinery until he is behind Tex's shoulder. He is shorter
than Tex and he must stand on his toes to see into the
boy's open belly.

"Whatcha got?" he asks, and Tex describes the
mushy feel of the back side of the liver. The older man
nods in agreement. Stellate fracture of the liver.

"How do you manage this problem?" the senior man
asks.

Tex says the first step is to extend the incision up
through the diaphragm and into the chest so the damage
can be seen. Then a decision must be made about how
best to control the bleeding.

The attending surgeon nods and asks Tex if he would
like to proceed. Tex would. It was the craving to operate
that had lured him East into the sleet and smog belt.

The attending surgeon moves in to put pressure on
the liver and Tex puts his hand out for a scalpel. The

scrub nurse lays it in his palm and the blade cuts across the rib cage, undulating over the bones.

"Rib cutter," he says, when the flesh is open. He takes the large pincers in both hands. The cutting jaws make a liquid crunching noise as they bite through the living bone. In a moment the chest wall can be pulled back to reveal a spongy lung that rises and falls in rhythm with the Engstrom. The knife parts the tough diaphragm and the attending surgeon lifts the liver up, and then they can see the starburst deceleration wound, where the liver, flying forward, burst on impact.

"Pressure is 90," says the anesthesiologist.

"Beep, beep," says the monitor, "be-beep, beep, be-beep."

Suddenly, the heart monitor is the loudest sound in the operating room.

"This is where he arrests," Tex says, his voice flat. "Come on, Jehovah. Come on, pay attention."

Tex steps back a few inches. There's nothing he can do. A patient this age could survive one arrest, and the boy did that. Then he had to withstand Tex cutting him open, and he did that, too. But another arrest . . . Tex would try. Already, the brain is too short of oxygen. Even if he restarted the heart, the brain might emerge badly damaged and the patient a vegetable. Or if the brain doesn't die and the patient isn't a vegetable, his immune system will fail and he'll die that way. Tex couldn't prove any of this, but he knows it. Even at the trauma unit there is a limit somewhere, and a surgeon learns to sense its proximity.

The colony of cells that composes the human body

is resilient. It can absorb frightening physical trauma and endure the chemical aftershocks. Short of oxygen and choked on their own metabolic wastes, the cells somehow make do. But in the end there is a breakpoint, a last straw, a final event that tips the balance away from survival. Then, the surgeon is helpless.

The terminal struggle more directly challenges the anesthesiologist, who administers a series of drugs to the faltering patient.

"Beep," the monitor goes, skipping. "Beep-beep, beep, beep."

The individual cell has its individual requirements, which vary from organ to organ, but they hold the basic processes in common. In the end, it's a question of fuel. Men die in shock, but each cell dies in an energy crisis.

The struggle centers on a small cellular organelle called a mitochondrion. The mitochondria are fuel refineries that use sugar and oxygen to produce an energy-rich compound called ATP, or adenosine triphosphate. The mitochondrion uses what ATP it needs to keep itself in good running order and gives the surplus to the surrounding cell. This leftover is the gasoline of life, and when it is no longer available, the cell shuts down forever.

Cells die all the time, and are replaced, but in the colony of cells that make up Tex's young patient, mass extinction seems about to occur. The strongest cells survive the longest and could eventually replace their dead neighbors, but few cells of the body are capable of surviving alone. They need oxygen, nutrients, marching orders from the hormone-producing cells, coordinating signals from the brain. The human body is, above all, an organization.

"Beep, beep, be-beep, beep . . . "

Finally, somewhere, one critical cell can die, disrupting a function that, in turn, is necessary for the survival of still more cells. Those cells die, producing a malfunction that destroys a critical organ. . . .

"Beep, beep, beep, beep-beep . . . beep . . . beep . . . "

The anesthesiologist works rapidly. He injects drugs directly into the tubes that carry blood and other liquid into the vessels. Cardiac medication is injected into the hollow tube that twists and turns through the veins and finally opens at a major intake to the heart.

The scrub nurse's right hand rests on the defibrillators.

The pressure is 100.

Tex focuses his eyes on the operating room clock and listens to the slow, irregular beeping. The second hand turns slowly, round and round. The heart should not be slowing. When a patient is in shock and his blood pressure drops, the heart should race to make up the difference, to pump harder, harder. When the heart doesn't race in shock, it's because it can't.

"Blood pressure is 105," the anesthesiologist calls out.

His face is wet with sweat. The respirator runs quietly and the heart monitor beeps a little faster now; the ear can't tell the difference but the sensors can. The blood pressure is 110. The scrub nurse closes her eyes. The blood pressure is 115. Much more slowly, it continues to rise, 117, 117, 119, 118, 120.

"The heartbeat is firming," says the anesthesiologist.

"Thank God," the nurse says.

Smile wrinkles appear above Tex's mask. "Naw," he says. "It was me and Jehovah."

"Not necessarily in that order," the nurse says, haughtily.

"Jehovah ain't board certified in surgery," Tex says. "But I am."

He steps forward, reaching his left hand behind the liver, pulling it up to expose the tear on the underside. Liver fractures are a surgeon's nightmare. The soft tissue is full of arteries, veins, bile ducts and other channels, and it oozes blood and chemicals at the touch of a scalpel. And a liver tear is impossible to patch up. It's like trying to sew Jello.

The damaged lobe of liver is like a peninsula extending away from the central mass of hepatic tissue. Tex could simply cut off the damaged portion, but then the raw stump would bleed and ooze, and the discharge would be a breeding ground for bacteria.

The solution is to be found in the problem. The liver is the consistency of a warm cantaloupe, so it doesn't need to be cut. Instead, Tex mashes the tissue between his thumb and forefinger. It squashes easily, but the vessels that run through it do not. Those he clamps.

Later he will tie a suture around every clamped vessel, then cut the lobe away. That will be a while, though. There are a lot of vessels, at least fifty, and the going is slow. Tex pinches and clamps, pinches and clamps, and the accumulating hemostats click against one another with every movement of the surgeon's strong hands. As he works, the bleeding tapers off and the patient improves visibly.

"He's pinkin' up real good," Tex says, pleased, when color begins to return to the patient's skin.

It is the circulating nurse who sees a few drops of urine dripping into the bag.

Outside, the orthopedic surgeon scrubs at the deep sink. He'll fix the broken leg now. It has to be done now. The patient would never survive a second anesthesia.

12

—

IF A YOUNG SURGEON WITH A DREAM IS DESTINED to irritate older ones whose dreams are dead, he also exerts a powerful charisma on other young visionaries. It was inevitable that Dr. McAslan, the hospital's best anesthesiologist, would form a partnership with the best heart surgeon. Elizabeth Scanlan admired Cowley because he was, well, Cowley.

"He made me just flip right out," she remembers now, smiling at her one-time innocence. "At that particular time, geez, that was probably about '52 or '53, heart surgery was a brand-new thing. Here I was a hick nurse, and I can remember I always wanted to meet him . . . but I never saw him. I only saw this big crowd of people around him.

"One day I finally saw him and evidently he liked my looks. I think he caught notice of me because I always used to have my cap on crooked."

For whatever reason, Cowley noticed. He had motive enough. In those days nurses were scarce and well-trained young ones who were still awed by doctors were downright rare. Cowley had need of loyal nurses.

Would Liz like to become a cardiac care nurse? As a matter of fact, Liz said, she would.

One of the job's biggest attractions was that Cowley appreciated nurses. During the long nights he'd spent sitting at the bedside of dying heart surgery patients, he'd learned what a good nurse can accomplish. Too often the doctor wasn't present when a crisis occurred, and crises don't wait. When they do, the snowball grows. A nurse, he decided, should be a stand-in for the doctor.

"I really liked the way Dr. Cowley worked with the nurses," Liz says. "He was the only physician in the whole hospital who took the nurses along on rounds with him. And it really intrigued me to find out that a heart surgeon, one in a million, was spending a significant amount of his time making rounds with nurses."

Liz soon became Cowley's death lab research assistant. In time she would become his confidante, his chief nurse and the second most powerful person in the Shocktrauma unit.

For his part the heart surgeon, who would one day receive a necktie emblazoned with "male chauvinist pig" from his nursing staff, was astonished to find a nurse so useful.

"Here was a woman, not another doctor . . . a woman with a different discipline from mine but whom I could work with, who was totally productive. She was the first person I had ever worked with who could take all these stupid goddamned ideas of mine and three hours later have me something on paper saying this is what you want . . . A, B, C, D . . . I'm a terrible outliner and she was an organizer."

Liz helped Cowley open the death lab in 1961, and within a year they had put a solid statistical foundation under the dream. If they could begin treating an accident victim within the first hour, and if they could control the oscillations of secondary shock, they could save many thousands of lives.

For a time they toyed with the idea of mobile operating rooms in tractor-trailer trucks. They could be stationed in areas where the accident rate was high and, when someone was seriously injured, the medical rig would meet the ambulance halfway.

The preferred solution, however, would be the one the army used. Helicopters. But choppers were awesomely expensive and neither Liz nor Cowley could imagine getting their hands on that kind of money.

That was the general state of affairs when the next disciple appeared in 1963. She was Sandra Bond, a new graduate from the medical secretaries' school in rural Hagerstown, who had come to the big city for her first professional experience.

As soon as she arrived at the University of Maryland, a senior secretary took her aside. She was going to work for Dr. Cowley, right? Oh, wow! The older woman was sympathetic.

The heart surgeon's rapport with nurses did not translate into a similar relationship with secretaries, Sandy learned. His temper was legend in the typing pool.

"If Dr. Cowley yells at you," the woman told Sandy, "don't be frightened."

The warning was supposed to be reassuring, but it wasn't. "I thought, oh, God, if he ever yells at me that'll be the end. I was scared to death. I was just absolutely petrified."

The older woman stopped by Sandy's office every day to inquire about her mental health, but Sandy was fine. Cowley, for the moment, was on his best behavior. By the time he finally got around to yelling at Sandy, she had gained the confidence that goes with experience and she surprised them both; she yelled back. In the seventeen years since, she and Cowley have institutionalized yelling as a means of formal communication at the trauma unit.

Sandy, like Liz, became Cowley's colleague, ally and confidante. Working late night after night, never marrying, she learned to share the heart surgeon's worries and dreams. She organized his schedule, nagged him to take his vitamins and move to a safer apartment and jealously protected him from the world at large.

On one legendary occasion the governor's chief of staff tried unsuccessfully for three days to reach Cowley, but Sandy judged Cowley to be too busy and refused to put the calls through. When he finally reached Cowley, the man began the conversation by demanding that Sandy be fired. Cowley told him to go to hell.

Cowley, Liz and Sandy junked the tractor-trailer trauma unit plan when they figured out a way to get helicopters. The general scheme was to co-opt the state police.

The police force, Cowley had discovered, wanted helicopters to monitor traffic and chase criminals. Senior state police officials went to the federal government, but the Washington bureaucrats didn't think the idea was cost effective.

The trauma team at the University of Maryland proposed to share those helicopters, dramatically increasing their usefulness. For their part, state police officers agreed to let Cowley train troopers as medics. There would be a medic in each helicopter at all times, and medical assignments would have absolute priority over law enforcement functions.

With that arrangement in mind, the Department of Transportation agreed to buy Maryland an air force.

The Department of Health, Education and Welfare was also impressed with Cowley's dream, and in 1963 agreed to give him $800,000 . . . half of what a centralized trauma unit would cost to build.

It would be a unit that would become the prototype for all others in the world, a five-story building designed specifically for trauma medicine, in effect a death lab expanded to twelve beds.

The first floor above the basement would be the admitting area, a twenty-first-century accident room in which every possible life-support system would stand waiting. The doctors, nurses and attendants required to save a dying patient would be present twenty-four hours a day. Two stories above, a trauma lab would stand ready to produce blood-study results in a matter of minutes.

The dying patient would go first to the admitting area, where the medical team would pull him back from the edge of death. Then he would be moved to the operating room for the repair of his injuries and, finally, he would go up to the fourth floor.

The fourth floor would contain the life machine, a twelve-bed unit designed to incorporate all the knowledge gained in the death lab. There the trauma teams would use the most modern technology to damp down oscillations and combat metabolic chaos.

It would be Cowley's dream come true, but his university had some serious reservations.

It was nice that the federal government was going to pay half, but where was the university supposed to get the rest of the money? Would some of it come out of the department of urology? How about pediatrics, becoming compromised by falling birthrates? Already, professors of gynecology and obstetrics were having a tough time explaining why their budgets shouldn't be trimmed to match the dwindling patient load.

And what if Cowley were right? What if he could save half the dying motorists? If he did, twelve beds wouldn't be enough. A hundred beds might not be enough. And where were those beds supposed to come from? The question aroused the territorial instincts that underlie so many academic power struggles.

The administrative gears that were supposed to process Cowley's request for a matching $800,000 slowed to a near halt. The university began to equivocate about the money. Cowley seethed at the delay.

As four years passed and nothing happened, the heart surgeon began pounding on desks and insisting that people were dying needlessly. As his dream turned into a crusade, the thrust of his arguments began to shift, and now, more and more, he argued for the right of dying motorists to competent medical treatment.

His pleas for a better medical system won admirers

85

among laymen, but the desks he pounded on belonged to doctors, and they viewed the matter differently. Cowley was seen as an empire-builder, pure and simple.

Dr. Schnaper, the Shocktrauma psychiatrist, said that by the time he joined the Cowley team he had heard the empire-builder accusation so many times, and from so many people, that he believed it.

"But I've come to see that it can be explained more simply. This is his baby. He created it. Ain't nobody gonna touch his baby. Nobody's gonna interfere with its growth, and he'll fight like a tigress. At times he almost invites a fight, but what he is is an over-anxious mother with a baby.

"I would say he's a brilliant, creative genius. He's innovative, and he's a pain in the ass. That's a psychiatric diagnosis."

Cowley diagnosed it differently. He didn't make the crisis, there already was one. People were dying.

People *were* dying, of course, and eventually the university paid the matching money. But because of the construction delay, the helicopters started flying before the unit opened, and Cowley, limited by the size of the death lab, started scrounging bed space from other departments.

He got the beds he needed. When a doctor is in possession of a dying patient it's very difficult for a nurse or an administrator to deny him the use of an empty bed. The encroachment further alarmed the University of Maryland doctors.

When the unit finally opened in 1969, the administration refused to pay for the personnel required to put the operating rooms into service. Otherwise, though, the unit was operational and the helicopter medics began going after patients in earnest. Hostilities commenced immediately.

One of the most serious incidents involved a patrolling state trooper who discovered a serious accident and radioed for a helicopter. A local ambulance squad arrived before the chopper did and was determined to take the patient to the nearest hospital.

The discussion turned contentious, then ugly. The ambulance team attempted to rush the trooper but stopped, astonished, when the officer drew his revolver. He held the volunteer ambulance medics at gunpoint until the helicopter landed and departed safely with the patient.

The motorist survived, but that and other incidents provoked an uproar in volunteer firehouses across the state. The collective outrage of the volunteers had immediate political consequences.

Volunteer firemen in Maryland, like those in many other states, are a potent constituency. Their organizations, kept healthy by a constant schedule of well-attended bingo games, cakewalks, crab feasts and flea markets, often play critical roles in the rise and fall of politicians. The late Maryland Governor J. Millard Tawes found it expedient to begin his first gubernatorial campaign in the state's volunteer firehouses.

And who, the volunteers asked, was this Cowley fellow? Who was he to tell them how to run their ambulances? Who was he to say they were poorly equipped and ill-trained, more experienced in parades than modern emergency medicine? What did he *really* want?

Emergency room doctors, who perceived Cowley as

trying to steal their patients, told the ambulance volunteers that the heart surgeon was a megalomaniac and an empire builder. The rumor went around that it was all part of a plan to replace the volunteers with paid men, thereby defusing the political force of the volunteers. The vollies believed it.

"No goddamned helicopter's going to land in my county," one county fire chief boasted to his men. Emergency rooms that got multiple trauma patients kept them, transferring them to the trauma unit only after repeated attempts to resuscitate them had failed. By that time, of course, it was too late.

The University of Maryland, like many large state schools, was perennially sensitive to political breezes. Life got tougher for Cowley and his team. The operating rooms sat dark and empty as university officials funded empty pediatrics beds while leisurely studying Cowley's proposals. In the meantime, the worst trauma patients had to be rolled from the admitting area, down a block of hallway, and up seven floors to the university's central operating suites. Sometimes there was an OR available and sometimes there wasn't.

"Our operating rooms were totally equipped, ready to go, and left empty for three years," Cowley remembers. "And in one eight-month period I lost fifteen patients just trying to get them from here over to the main hospital and up to the operating rooms."

One of Cowley's early students, Dr. David Boyd, later rose to become the federal government's top-ranking emergency care expert. As chief of the Division of Emergency Medical Services in the federal health bureaucracy, he has attempted to protect and nourish the other trauma units that, based on Cowley's numbers, have arisen across the country. In each case, he says, there has been strong and often bitter opposition from local medical and ambulance groups.

"They'll give you seventy-two reasons why it can't be done. Where's your data? It won't work! You'll get sued for malpractice. Patient stealing. Communism. Anything.

"You're breaking the doctor-patient relationship, that's the first thing you get from the county medical society. There's a whole list of goddamned things, all of which are smoke. Pure smoke.

"In many places it's still a tug-of-war between the ambulance and the helicopter. Some places there's still some kind of payola going on . . . real payola or not-so-real payola. Somebody's got coffee or nurses or pizza, or something that drags those (ambulance) guys into the 'right' hospital. And that's not always the trauma center.

"Let me tell you, trauma is the most severe, the most complex disease entity you'll ever see. And it lands on your doorstep when you don't want it, when you don't expect it. If you do not have a program ready to respond to that, you are killing patients—I don't give a shit what you say."

Though Cowley's political troubles soon began to threaten the very survival of the trauma unit, his pioneering medical practices made him a hero among young doctors. A steady stream of the country's best surgeons-in-training competed for fellowships at Shock-trauma. Of equal importance, dozens of aggressive nurses applied for jobs in Cowley's life machine.

Allies came from outside the medical profession as well. John Ashworth, the son of a prominent local surgeon, became the unit's administrator in 1971. As soon as Cowley, Liz, Sandy and McAslan discovered his ability to manipulate the bureaucratic machine, Ashworth became a member of the team.

Dr. Schnaper joined the group almost by accident in 1972. Cowley had urged him time after time—as he urged almost everyone—to come see his unit. Dr. Schnaper specialized in the psychology of the dying patient and he figured a trauma patient probably didn't do much thinking, and less communicating. Visiting Cowley's unit was somewhere near the bottom of his priority list.

The Saturday finally came, however, when the psychiatrist was bored enough to make the visit. He ambled over, intending to remain only a few minutes. Instead, he stayed for hours. He hadn't anticipated the tension, and it was the tension that hooked him.

"This place is a gold mine," he says, many years later. "Not just the patients, the docs. The doctors, the nurses, everybody."

Dr. Schnaper, as a scientist and a people-watcher, wanted access to the everyday life-and-death drama of the shocktrauma unit. In return, he became instantly responsible for the mental health of Cowley, his patients and everybody else who had anything to do with Cowley's baby.

Often the heart surgeon, brooding over his locked operating rooms or his chronic bed shortage, would call Dr. Schnaper late at night . . . just to talk. Dr. Schnaper was usually tolerant.

"Cowley," he reflects, "is a mold of contradictions. He's a genius, but he's stupid. He is very sophisticated, but he's a little boy. He's warm and generous, and he's a bastard. He's a nice guy and he's a pain in the ass. And he is a very lonely man."

13

THE VENDING MACHINES OFFER FRECKLES A
choice between a packaged cheese sandwich, a plastic-
looking hot dog and a can of Dinty Moore Beef Stew.
Deciding that the cheese sandwich is the least of the
proffered evils, she feeds her quarters into the slot. A
chocolate bar, a package of cheese crackers and an extra
pack of cigarettes go into the brown leather purse that
hangs over her shoulder. Then eight nickels for a can
of Hawaiian Punch. Sandwich in one hand and soft
drink in the other, she walks slowly back to the unit.
As she approaches the nurses' lounge adjacent to the
critical care recovery unit, a male voice calls her name.

Freckles stops to lean against the SYSCOM door
jamb. The operator grins at her and asks what she's
doing back on the fourth floor. "I thought you'd turned
in your passport when you moved downstairs," the man
says. Freckles shakes her head no, scratching her nose
with the Hawaiian Punch can. It's just for a couple of
weeks. So Lisa can go on vacation. After that she'll be
down in Admitting permanently.

"Admitting's nice," she says. "You get to sit down once in a while." Then she walks on to the nurses' lounge and sinks into an armchair. The only other occupant of the room is a uniformed city policeman who looks up as Freckles enters and then returns to the six thumbnail-sized squares of newsprint in front of him.

The evening paper lies, demolished, on the floor, with the pencil-marked daily Jumble folded neatly on top. The paper squares have been carefully torn, by hand, from the margins of that page, and on each square the policeman has printed a letter.

The squares of paper lie on a clear spot in the center of the coffee table. A clutter of crushed cigarette packs, full ashtrays and empty food containers are piled at both ends of the coffee table and a banana peel, neatly rolled and wrapped with surgical tape, lies in the center of a dirty paper plate. The policeman concentrates on the arrangement in front of him. The letters spell H-E-M-A-P-T.

Freckles watches him as he watches the pieces of paper. "One of the nurses try to escape again?" she finally asks, taking a bite from the sandwich. The cop looks up from the letters and smiles.

"I wouldn't blame you for trying," he says. "I wouldn't want to work in there. You got a real badass tonight, though . . . if he makes any trouble for you, I'm right here." He goes back to his puzzle and Freckles chews quietly on her sandwich.

The cop rearranges the letters to spell first THEMPA, then PHEAMT, then ETMAPH.

"He feels for you," the cop says.

"What?" Freckles snaps, shaken from her reverie.

"He feels for you. It's the clue. It's something you can spell with A-M-P-H-E-T, and the clue is, 'He feels for you.' "

"Oh," says the nurse, around a mouth of sandwich. "I never work those things. They drive me nuts."

The cop transposes two letters and stares some more. There is a rustle of leather as he changes position. Handcuffs, nightstick, a can of Mace, two cartridge pouches and a service revolver hang from his belt. The handle of a blackjack protrudes from his back pocket.

The arrangement MATHEP doesn't suggest anything to the cop, so he tries EPHAMT. That doesn't help either, nor does AEPHTM.

"What kind of badass?" Freckles asks.

"A badass full of buckshot right now," the officer replies. "He tried to kill two PO-lice. If he makes any trouble, I'm right here. He won't though. They tell me he's pretty sick." The cop grins at Freckles.

"Thanks," she says. "I feel better now."

Her sandwich finished, she downs the last of the Hawaiian Punch and walks out the door. In the hallway there is a supply shelf. She replaces her paper cap and struggles out of her pink wraparound gown, throwing it on top of a heaping laundry cart.

Inside SYSCOM, the operator talks into a microphone and scribbles notes. He raises his eyebrows at Freckles as she walks by and she waves at him through the window, continuing to walk toward the line of red tiles that separate the trauma recovery unit from the rest of the world. The policeman can't follow the nurse across that line, nor can the SYSCOM operator: the risk of infection is too great. Visitors are barred from seeing the men and women who lie naked on the brink of death.

Freckles's shoes make a small squeaking noise against the spotless tile as she walks around the foot of the raised platform, the island that dominates the critical care unit. The pupils of her eyes contract, adjusting to the intense illumination that emanates from the ceiling and bounces off the tile and stainless steel, washing out shadows. From the other side of the island, a male voice bellows in pain. Freckles smiles and waves at a clerk who looks down from the island.

From behind Freckles, an alarm beeps frantically and a female voice calls out, "Got that!" The beeping stops. Freckles turns the corner of the island without looking back. Cubicle eight is on the other side.

Number eight, like most of the other cubicles, is a three-sided space facing the island. The man lies, feet outward, in an intensive care bed. His midsection is dotted with purple puncture marks, and an ugly surgical scar runs from his breastbone to his groin. The incision is closed with heavy, plastic-covered wire.

Another red line stretches across the entrance to the cubicle, warning unnecessary medical personnel to keep their distance. Freckles steps across it without hesitation. Lisa, bending over a metal-jacketed medical record book, looks up, her face friendly. "Hi Freck, you're wonderful," she says, turning toward the patient. "Walter? Walter, your new nurse is here. Freckles, this is Walter."

Lisa completes her note, picks up the chart and walks with Freckles to the island. They sit side by side at a cabinet overlooking the unit, spreading the paperwork before them.

There is the sound of a nurse's hands slapping loudly and rapidly against flesh, followed by a subdued, painful cough.

"I hate to do this to you," Lisa says, "but he just spiked a one-oh-two. We're gonna have to do the whole fever pack. I'll stay and help you."

Freckles gazes down at the patient. Buckshot. Perforations of the bowel. Infection. A fever protocol is a lot of work, but a man can't pack a suitcase.

"No, go on home. I'll do it. I thought you had someone in nine, too."

"I did, but they moved him out about an hour ago. Your admission will be in nine. Was he really a Jehovah's Witness?"

"I think he's a Baptist now. Walter doesn't look all that bad to me. I thought he was in worse shape. . . ."

Lisa laughs aloud. "You must have talked to the cop? You did. Well, for two days they've been wanting to put chains on him. He doesn't need chains. I don't think he's going to run away."

Turning abruptly to business, Lisa opens the chart and begins reciting in a monotone. Walter's a thirty-one-year-old black male, with a history of multiple gunshot wounds to the legs and abdomen.

Lisa stops and looks at Freckles. "I think he shot two of them. That's why they don't like him."

Freckles jots notes on a paper towel. "Where are the cops?" she asks.

"Mercy, I think. They weren't serious. His last blood series was four hours ago, and he came back 15.2 and

96

49. His gases are beautiful: 169, 7.41, 39 and 99. The only problem is the fever spike I just got. He has a wife, named Viola, and she's a real bitch. I talked to her earlier and she may call back. She called yesterday morning at three o'clock and there was a lot of music in the background. She didn't sound sober. Walter said to tell her he was asleep. Let me help you do the fever pack."

"No," Freckles says, firmly. "You go home and do the suitcase pack. Get out of here. Have a good time."

"Thanks," Lisa says. "G'bye." She slips off the seat and disappears down the far steps of the island.

Freckles's eyes rest on Walter. His heartbeat jumps steadily across the monitor above him. Somewhere in his body, bacteria are growing. Somewhere, a rubber foot squeaks as it slides across tile. Contaminated gloves slap noisily against the side of a trash pail. Few of the noises are loud, but there are many of them and each one has a meaning familiar to Freckles. It is sometimes pleasant having a patient who can talk.

"Hello, Walter," Freckles says. "I hear you have a temperature."

"Oh mama," the patient says back. "Does that mean you're gonna stick me?"

"Yep," Freckles says brightly.

"Is the Man still out there waiting for me?"

"Yep."

"Then I guess I got no choice but to get stuck, huh?"

"Yep."

Freckles reaches for a large syringe and two small test tubes with brightly colored rubber caps on them, a red and a purple. Walter is in no position to fight, since his left wrist is securely tied with gauze to the left railing of the bed and the right one is likewise attached to the other side. His left hand is tied to protect the sensor that enters the radial artery in his forearm, and his right hand is tied to protect the glassware and the nurses from Walter. Freckles chats cordially with her patient, making small talk as she checks to see that all his intravenous lines are functioning properly.

A Shocktrauma cubicle is a confining space, especially when it is occupied by two young people, one healthy and the other at the edge of death. The nurses learn to relate openly and honestly with the people in their care, partly for the good of the patient and partly to help the nurses cope. The situation is simpler in Walter's case, since he will probably live and, since he has no chest injuries, he's not on a respirator and is able to talk. Also willing. Talking sometimes helps the pain, and the trauma nurses are much better company than the guards in the prison wing of the hospital, where he will go after he leaves the Critical Care Recovery Unit.

Walter stares at the bottles and tubes overhead as the nurse palpates a vein on the inside of his right forearm. "You got nice veins, Walter. Are you as bad as they say you are?"

"Naw," Walter replies. "I just got bad luck. That other nurse says I ought to see a shrink. I get confused sometimes. Ow. Ow. OW!"

The blood wells up in the syringe. When she has enough, Freckles removes the needle and presses a sterile alcohol pad against the puncture mark. "When do you get confused?"

"Every time I get the money."

"What money?" Freckles inquires, absently, as she distributes the syringe of blood into the two tubes.

"I usually make them put it in paper bags. The first time was in a liquor store. When I got the bag in my hand I got real confused. They almost got me and I dropped the money. This last time was worse, though."

Freckles turns and looks down at Walter. "You mean you get confused when you're sticking places up?"

"Yeah," Walter admits, smiling. "That's why I want to see a shrink. That other nurse says shrinks can treat things like that."

Moving to the foot of the bed, Freckles bends down to collect specimens from the bag at the end of Walter's catheter, and from the graduated cylinder at the end of the plastic drain tube that the surgeons left in the belly.

The fever protocol requires Freckles to take a dozen samples of blood, mucus, sputum, urine and other material. Each sample will be examined several times with a variety of different techniques. Doctors can better prescribe an antibiotic if they know what kind of bacteria they're dealing with. There is little room for error in the therapy, since a minor infection in a trauma patient can initiate an explosive growth of poisonous organisms in the bloodstream. Blood infection, called septicemia, is the most common cause of death in the CCRU.

"I hear you shot somebody," Freckles says, shaking the rectal thermometer. Specific orders on taking Walter's temperature were given earlier in the day, after he responded to a wave of pain by biting an oral thermometer in half. Walter sighs.

"That was later," he says. "It started out I was in this grocery store and the front doors were locked. They were closing up. Everybody was real polite . . . oh, man, that's COLD . . . anyway they put the money in paper sacks and put the little paper sacks in a big paper sack and gave it to me. That's when I got confused. I thought I was going out the back way, but I got lost in the vegetables and when I finally found the door I ran through, and you know where I was? I was in the motherfuckin' meat locker! Before I could figure out where I was they slammed the door on me and locked it."

Freckles withdraws the thermometer. It reads 102.2. "I thought you shot somebody, Walter," she says again.

"I didn't mean to," Walter says, looking away. "I was just trying to get loose. This fool turns his back and it was like offering me his gun. It wasn't even strapped into the holster. So I tried to leave and got confused all over again. Then they started shooting at me. That really confused me. This big dude with this big shotgun tried to kill me."

"He didn't, though, did he?" Freckles says, lifting the dressing away from the right arm, where the arterial sensor dips into the flesh. The lines running into the body are obvious places for infection to begin, especially when the immune system is wiped out by shock. Twice already, Walter's fever has risen and each time he began to slip into septic shock, but twice the doctors and nurses pulled him back. Freckles sees no pus, so she replaces the dressing with a fresh one.

A fever pack is a lot of work. A half hour passes, and Freckles still works steadily. She performs adequately, but less efficiently than she had fourteen hours earlier, when she reported for work in the admitting area. The fever pack should take thirty minutes. Freckles will be lucky to finish in forty.

The painful examination of his wounds and the multiple needle pricks make Walter irritable. The third time a needle appears he begins struggling and cursing loudly. Freckles talks soothingly to him, and when the fever protocol is done she gives him a shot of morphine. That quiets him down, and starts him talking again, complaining about his bad luck.

"Maybe you ought to retire from the business," Freckles suggests.

"Yeah," Walter says. "Wouldn't that be nice. Retire and go somewhere. Buy a farm."

"That would be nice," says Freckles. "But the way I feel right now, I'd settle for a nice quiet emergency room someplace."

Freckles looks up as a familiar form passes the cubicle, pauses in mid-stride and stops. "What are you doing here?" the senior nurse asks, puzzled. "Where's Lisa?"

Freckles explains why she relieved Lisa. It was the only thing to do, she says. "Can you imagine going on vacation and having your boyfriend pack?"

The senior nurse looks more worried than impressed.

" . . . men can't pack," Freckles adds, lamely.

"Man, I can pack good," Walter says from the bed. "I pack tens and twenties and ones and fives in brown paper bags real good. When I buy my farm, I'll buy you an emergency room and we'll both retire."

The nurse stands, staring, at Freckles. Freckles turns

magenta. "I . . . I . . ." her voice trails off. The stare continues a moment longer.

"Yeah," the woman says. "Whatever. I gotta go."

Freckles turns back to her patient. "Thanks, Walter. You're a real pal."

Later, when Walter is asleep, Freckles goes to the nurses' lounge for a cigarette and a cup of coffee. The cop is still busy with his Jumble, which now spells MA-TEPH.

"Have any trouble with that guy?" the cop asks.

"No."

"Look," the cop says. "I been thinking. It'd be a lot safer for you in there if you'd let me put irons on him."

"He's in a coma, for Chrissakes!" Freckles snaps.

"Oh." The cop goes back to his Jumble.

Freckles sits for a few moments with her eyes closed. Then she puts out her cigarette in what's left of her coffee, gets up and walks to the door. There she turns, comes back and stands over the cop's shoulder. She looks at the letters for a moment, shaping a word with her mouth. She reaches down and rearranges the letters to read EMPATH, hesitates enough to hear the cop's frustrated grunt and exits without a word.

14

JEFF KNEW THE SHIFT WAS GOING TO BE HEC-
tic when he arrived shortly before midnight and found
that there were already two cases down in Admitting.
So he is grateful for the ten-minute stroll over to University Hospital's blood bank. The chore provides an
opportunity to worry over a mathematical formula he
needs to understand for a seminar Monday. Since Jeff
became an orderly at the trauma unit he has earned a
bachelor's degree in mathematics and will soon have
his master's.

At the blood bank Jeff hands a stack of requisitions
across the counter to the hematology technician. The
two men know one another well, since Shocktrauma
uses most of University Hospital's blood supply. For
that matter, the unit uses half of all the blood that the
Red Cross collects in Baltimore.

"How were the flounder?" Jeff asks, as the technician
leafs through the papers on a clipboard. The technician
was fishing yesterday. He's the only person Jeff knows
who goes fishing in February, and he listens, uncon-

vinced, to the story that follows, his eyebrows going up when the man spreads his hands to indicate the unlikely length of the one that got away. Stellate fracture. One of the patients in Admitting is a stellate fracture, and that means a lot of blood, a lot of everything. He'll come up to the unit with tubes and lines and drains and bottles and bags, the works.

The hematology technician puts the bags of blood and a large empty plastic sack on the countertop. Each small bag of blood components has a red coding sticker on it. The code is ATX 5975. The same combination of letters and numbers appears on Jeff's requisitions.

The technician picks up the top bag and examines the code while Jeff, holding the requisition form, reads it out loud. The technician nods and hands Jeff the bag while, with the other hand, he accepts the requisition. This time the technician reads the number and Jeff examines the bag. The routine finished, Jeff puts the bag in the plastic sack. The technician sets the requisition aside and picks up a second bag.

"ATX 5975," Jeff reads. The process is repeated for each of the four bags.

"I got some more for Admitting," the technician says, filing the requisition forms. "You want to take those too?"

Jeff hesitates. It requires consideration. He doesn't have the requisitions, so he can't cross-check the numbers, and if he doesn't cross-check he's breaking protocol. That's not to be done lightly.

On the other hand, Admitting is pretty busy and if they have to send someone over separately for the blood that will slow down the admitting process slightly. Delay carries a risk too, in Admitting. Besides, the blood is type O, and almost anybody can receive type O without a reaction. The risk is slight and Jeff will be very careful.

"Sure," he says. The technician puts the blood on the counter.

On the way back to the trauma unit, Jeff stops briefly to scribble an equation on a folded piece of paper he pulls out of his scrub suit pocket. Juggling the blood bags awkwardly, he fiddles with the equation for a moment, shakes his head in disgust and draws a large X over the symbols. Replacing the paper, he continues on his way, muttering.

In the admitting area, Jeff puts the half-dozen bags of blood into the refrigerator. Painstakingly he notes the delivery on a chart and double checks the numbers. They match. From across the room the nurse trainee watches. She is impressed. She once worked six months in an operating room, and she never saw this much blood in a single day. In an emergency, blood was always available, usually not too far away. But it had to be located and maybe even driven across town. The taxi drivers helped out a lot, but the process took time.

The trainee remembers one occasion when a young surgeon doing a stomach resection discovered an undiagnosed aneurysm . . . the hard way. The surgeon was a good one and the patient lived, but in the process the operation consumed all the B positive blood that had been stored for another patient.

Unfortunately, that patient was an irritable contractor who donated money, sat on the hospital board and was terrified of needles. He had dreaded the surgery, avoided it for months, finally steeled himself for it . . .

and now? Incompetence! The surgery was delayed for twenty-four hours and the contractor spent the first of those hours screaming at the hospital president. The president had a long talk with the chief of surgery, and the chief of surgery delivered a scathing ten-minute dressing-down to the young surgeon. The surgeon listened until his chief was finished and then took a swing at him, abruptly ending his residency.

In the nurse trainee's experience, the same sort of thing happened every time a multiple trauma victim arrived. The blood supply was exhausted, the operating room schedule was demolished and it always ended with people refusing to talk to one another. It didn't do the patient much good, either.

Once, in that same hospital, a little black girl came in, in an ambulance. There was no warning, all of a sudden the patient was there. Dressed in a pinafore, of all things. The pinafore stuck in the trainee's mind. And the blood that pumped out of the severed arm.

The ambulance crew said the girl had been playing with an older brother in a freightyard, when one of the trains began to move. She had B negative blood. B negative isn't particularly rare and the hospital usually had several units on hand. But that day they had only one, and there had been no warning. The girl never came out of shock.

That hospital was generally unprepared for the dying toddler, and the staff knew it. The drills worked fine, but the real thing is always messier than planned drills, and the urgency affected people's reactions. The nurse trainee had stood for one unforgettable moment, watching the blood pump onto the pinafore. But the staff did the best it could with what it had, and the fact that there wasn't enough blood . . . bad luck. Thinking about things like that was unproductive.

But at the Baltimore trauma unit the team leader has no excuses. He's got blood. Equipment. Supplies. Veteran manpower. In minutes, he could muster enough of those resources to treat twelve dying patients. As every field commander knows, efficient logistics translate into time, and time is everything.

The depth of the trauma unit's logistics system is one of the reasons that Dr. David Boyd calls it the Taj Mahal of emergency medicine. As the nation's ranking trauma bureaucrat, it was Dr. Boyd who recommended to the Secret Service that the President, if injured in Washington, should be flown to the Shocktrauma unit in Baltimore.

Dr. Boyd worked for Cowley in the death laboratory and then moved on to Illinois to attempt to set up a trauma system there. But in Illinois, he ran into the same bitter opposition that had made him leave Baltimore. There were delays and accusations of patient-stealing. Doctors struggled for control of dying patients. When the call came from Washington, he said yes.

He didn't finish the job in Illinois, he admits. That state still has no trauma center to match the one in Maryland. But neither did he fail. He left Illinois with the country's second-best system, complete with trained medics, helicopter evacuation and formally designated hospital rooms, where the surgeons treat enough trauma to be competent at it.

In Washington, Dr. Boyd continued to be an outspoken advocate of Cowley-style emergency medicine and an unyielding opponent of the traditional nearest-hospital approach.

Once the trauma patient rolls into the emergency room, he argues, it's too late to make preparations. Either the emergency room is ready, or it's too late. It's too late to ask another hospital for blood, too late to wake up a surgeon and call him in, too late to buy an extra respirator, too late to look up procedures in a medical book . . . too late. Dr. Boyd is blunt. "If you've got a head plus chest plus belly injury and the best they can front is an on-call surgeon with four units of blood in the bank, you're dead, man."

It's the nature of Cowley's disease that the patient always arrives at the most inopportune moment, a Murphy's Law of trauma. Accidents occur at night and on weekends and holidays, when the most experienced surgeons aren't readily available. Neither are there any people available to open the operating room, run the X-ray equipment or perform the necessary blood tests.

To make matters worse, Cowley says, most serious accidents occur at the rural edge of suburbia or in the open countryside, where hospitals are far between and, usually, rather small. Many rural hospital emergency rooms are still supervised by registered nurses with a doctor on call. Nurses are generally forbidden by law to administer blood without orders from a doctor, even if the blood is there to give.

In the average 250-bed hospital, the arrival of a trauma patient often triggers pandemonium. It is an unusual event and some of the available personnel will hesitate. There is confusion over who has the key that locks the storage room that contains the piece of equipment that no one dreamed would be needed. One technician will have to be called in to run the X-ray machine and, perhaps, another to type the blood. The surgeon, when he arrives, may never have seen a case quite like this before and he needs the advice of a chest surgeon. In the meantime the patient's torn arteries may be pumping all his blood into his chest and abdominal cavities.

The trauma victim's odds are not necessarily much improved if he arrives at a small hospital at nine o'clock on Monday morning. Since senior doctors are available, the junior man in the emergency room is custom-bound to consult a general surgeon about the belly, the chest surgeon about the pierced lung, the orthopedic surgeon about the broken leg and the neurosurgeon on the matter of a slow pupil. Two of those experts are in the operating room and will be down in a few minutes. The eventual decision is often the correct one, but it comes too late. The patient didn't have enough blood, and he didn't have enough oxygen, but what he had least of was time.

But the medical community is a largely private one, and the failures are never advertised. Rarely is a hospital challenged on its handling of a trauma victim, and even more rarely does it challenge itself.

Cowley, Boyd and other trauma experts argue that the small hospitals in fact gain by avoiding the trauma patient. Not only does the patient often die, but what Dr. Boyd calls the Chinese fire drill that accompanies his demise wrecks the hospital schedule for a week. The operating room is a mess, the blood bank is depleted, the on-call personnel must receive extra pay and the men and women who were involved spend the day sullen and depressed. In fact, hospitals in Maryland, where emergency medical service systems have been available for a decade, are saving money and morale.

But the instinctive reaction of the hospital establishment is to fight the construction of trauma units. What happened in Maryland, Dr. Boyd says, happens everywhere. Why it happens is an open question.

Dr. Schnaper, the center's psychiatrist, thinks money plays a major role. After all, he says, most motorists are insured and the insurance pays off whether the patient lives or dies.

Dr. Boyd disagrees. He thinks the opposition boils down to a question of status and professional jealousy. He says hospital administrators on the make don't want to admit that their emergency rooms can't treat serious trauma. That deficiency, if it became general knowledge, might undermine the institution's image in the community and ultimately cut into the fund-raising plans.

The surgeons resist for a different set of reasons, he believes, and most of those reasons involve ego. They won't admit their limitations.

"You get some stone-head surgeons and they think they're trauma experts because they took care of the fuckin' train wreck thirteen years ago, when everybody croaked. Everybody's a goddamned traumatologist, right? They don't know what the hell we're talking about!"

There is also the suggestion that the medical establishment's reluctance has to do with the forceful abrasiveness of traumatologists in specific and surgeons in general. One hospital administrator, after working for a physician who fought Cowley's unit, finally departed in disgust with both sides. The way he explains it, surgeons are universally stubborn.

"After the operation is over, the surgeon has to close his eyes to the alternatives. It's the only way he can live with himself. If he loses a patient, he can't look back. If the patient lives, of course, then he made the right decisions. But once a surgeon makes a decision, right or wrong, he doesn't change his mind."

That interpretation is not far removed from the theory expounded by Freckles to the nurse trainee. It may all be a function of male territoriality.

Downstairs in the admitting area, the nurse trainee watches the neurosurgeon stand once more at the foot of the table to scrape his reflex hammer across the bottom of the unconscious girl's feet. It has been a long time since he shouted into Christine's ear. His left hand still on the girl's foot, the neurosurgeon makes his decision.

A short trip away, one of modern medicine's most sophisticated X-ray machines waits. Its operator polishes her fingernails while reading a manual. Carefully, she reaches for the ringing telephone.

The nurse trainee has never seen a CAT scanner before. Her hospital in Norfolk wanted one, but the local hospital review commission wouldn't let the administrator buy it. They said it was too complex a piece of equipment to be operated accurately by a medium-sized hospital.

As soon as the neurosurgeon hangs up the telephone, the trainee buttonholes him. Sure, he says. Come along.

15

———

FOR THREE HOURS, THE BOY'S BLOOD PRESSURE
remains steady at 145 while Tex bends over his exposed
abdomen, painstakingly pinching away bits of his liver,
clamping off the biological plumbing and tying, tying,
tying. Finally, the last bleeder tied, Tex stands back a
moment to flex his aching shoulders. Then he inspects
the liver once more, carefully, for any injury he might
have missed.

To protect the raw stump of the liver, Tex slices free
part of a small fatty flap that hangs over the bowel like
an apron. He arranges that over the exposed surface of
the liver and anchors it in place with two quick sutures.
Then he stitches up the diaphragm.

The surgical retreat halts for a moment while Tex
reaches over behind the patient's spleen and removes
the small piece of clean fabric he left there. There is a
small spot of blood.

Quickly he pulls the spleen forward and examines it
under the bright surgical lights. On the upper part of
the organ, where the arteries and veins connect, a small

drop of blood appears. Matter-of-factly, Tex teases the vessels apart, then clamps and ties them. The scalpel quickly severs the vessels and Tex drops the organ into a stainless steel tray. The clock has moved ahead ten minutes.

Again Tex steps back to flex his shoulders. "You go talk to the family," the attending surgeon says. "I'll do the closure." It is less an offer than a command.

The circulating nurse pulls off Tex's gloves and unfastens his gown. Outside the operating room, he stands at the scrub sink and washes and washes, his face exhausted and blank. In the lounge he pours himself a cup of coffee and sits down, alone in the room. Everybody's busy. Tex hunkers over the coffee, blowing on it, but doesn't drink. Finally he sets it down and walks through the pneumatic doors and into the admitting area to ask a nurse what his patient's name is. She says it's Larry, and sure, she'd be glad to go along.

In the hallway, Tex and the nurse wrap pink gowns around their sterile clothing. Tex stops suddenly as he starts to step aboard the elevator. "Hold it for me." He stoops to remove the blood-soaked paper booties, walks across the hallway and drops them into a trash can.

On the way down, Tex leans against one side of the elevator and looks at the nurse's feet, and she stands on the other side and looks at his. They walk around the corner to the waiting room, the nurse slipping in the door in front of Tex.

A man and a woman are sitting on the small, uncomfortable couch at the far end of the room. They appear to be in their middle forties. Another man with white hair sits in a chair. They all rise when they see Tex with the operating room mask still hanging from his neck. "Are you Larry's family?" Tex asks. The woman says yes. She is his mother, this is his father and that's his uncle.

"Your son is alive. But he's very critically injured."

"Thank God," the mother cries, throwing herself against her husband's shoulder and sobbing. The father whispers into the woman's ear. The uncle stares at Tex.

"I think everybody ought to sit down," the nurse finally says.

The mother, father and uncle sit side by side on the couch and Tex sits down in front of them. The nurse sits in a corner and watches as the woman takes a handkerchief from her husband and, using a tiny mirror from her purse, dabs at her eyes.

Tex sits with his elbows on the arms of the wooden chair, his hands clasped in front of him. He says he's just come from the operating room. "I have to be honest with you," he says. "I don't know whether he will survive or not."

"We know he's hurt bad," the father says. "His sister, Linda, told us. She was in the car too. She called us from the hospital. Another hospital, not here. That's how we found out."

Tex nods. "When he had his accident, it threw him forward and he broke some ribs, but that's not his most important injury."

Tex puts his hands against his chest and upper abdomen. "He must have gone into the steering wheel like this. He's got a broken leg, too, but the important thing is that he sustained a stellate . . . he tore an artery

114

in his liver. We stopped the bleeding now and he seems stable. But you have to know, he may not live."

"Can we see him?" the mother asks.

"No," says the nurse. "I'm afraid not. You see, he's in the operating room now, and from there he'll go to our critical care recovery unit, which is kept sterile. His primary nurse will call you as soon as he gets up there."

The family sits, silent.

"Was his sister badly injured?" the nurse asks.

"No," the uncle replies. "The doctor in the emergency room said she was just shook up, but he wanted to keep her tonight for observation."

"I don't know why the hell she let Larry get behind that wheel in the first place," the father complains. "She knows better than that. Larry's not even old enough for a driver's license."

Again, silence. Larry's mother picks up a brochure and stares at it without reading: most families, after a few hours in the little room, have read the visitors' orientation pamphlet many times, and this one is badly worn.

"The problem is that he almost bled to death while they were bringing him in," Tex says. "Actually they were remarkably fast, but he was bleeding so badly that his heart stopped just about the time he got here. We got it started again, but a cardiac arrest is like having a heart attack.

"And then we had to do intensive surgery, an exploratory, and then we removed one lobe of his liver to control the bleeding. He's got plenty of liver left, don't worry about that. His heartbeat and blood pressure are steady now."

"What can we do?" the mother wants to know.

The nurse answers. "I need to get some information from you. After that, the best thing you can do is go home and get some rest."

Tex stands up and the uncle follows him outside. The two men stand close and talk in low voices. Tex repeats that he just doesn't know. There is no way to tell, even to guess.

"But the best thing this boy's got going for him is that he's a boy. If this same thing had happened to you or me, we'd be dead. He's had the injury and on top of that he's had major surgery, and you have to figure honestly that that's an injury too. He's stable now, and at his age he might well survive. There'll be a critical post-operative period of about a day, and we'll watch him carefully. After that, maybe I can tell you more.

"The thing we're worried about right now, frankly, is infection. Shock . . . by that I mean losing your circulation . . . does a lot of things to you and one of them is knock down your immune system. He may bleed some more, too.

"After we get done in the operating room, he'll go up to the unit. If he survives, he'll be there for ten days to two weeks. You won't be able to see him during that time, because of the risk of infection. After that he'll move to 4-C, that's an intensive care unit. You'll be able to visit him there.

"But, you see, no matter what, this is going to take a long time. The best thing you can do is take his parents home and put them to bed. The nurse will give you some medication if you think they need it. Otherwise, if they can just go on with their lives as best they can, that's the best way."

The uncle nods as he listens. "Look," he says when Tex is done, "I'm not a Jehovah's Witness. I talked them into giving you permission to operate, and I guess I'm partly responsible. One thing I want to do is get my family doctor down here to look at Larry. He's a good man."

Tex hesitates, then answers carefully. "Have him give me a call if you like, that'd be fine, but I'm afraid he doesn't have privileges here. I'll be glad to explain everything to him, though. Take my word for it, I'm afraid you'll have to for the time being, that Larry is getting the finest medical care that's available anywhere in this country."

Tex watches the man carefully. He can see doubt, then acceptance. "Well," the uncle finally says, "I've heard of this place. I guess you're good enough."

When the man goes back into the waiting room the surgeon from Texas climbs the stairs, enters the admitting area and walks back toward the operating rooms. He doesn't cast a sidewise glance at the nude woman on the table or at the unfamiliar nurse who is shouting *Christine, Christine, can you hear me*, into her ear.

16

HANDLING A PENCIL AND PAPER WHILE HOLDING onto a sack of blood bags is a maneuver that requires practice, but Jeff has done it many times. Using the blood as a writing surface, he writes an equation down on the square of paper. This time he is pleased with the result. He smiles at the empty hallway. Walking past the laundry cart he removes the pink gown without stopping and flings it expertly on top of the heap. Humming softly he crosses the red line into the CCRU. "Who's got nine?" he inquires loudly as he reaches the far end of the island. Freckles acknowledges and Jeff informs her of the blood delivery. "And welcome back," he adds. Freckles, busy with Walter, grunts a reply.

Jeff works the midnight shift by choice, both because the hours allow flexibility in his school schedule and because many nights are slow enough to allow a little study. All those benefits are enough to compensate for the one inescapable routine that Jeff hates. The night shift attendants must change the Dispolexes.

A Dispolex is a brand of plastic container, one of which sits near the head of every trauma unit bed. Designed to contain two quarts of liquid, the Dispolex comes equipped with an upright top with tubing fittings. One tube runs to the vacuum outlet in the wall and the other ones lead to orifices, both natural and unnatural, in the body.

Patients almost always have nasogastric tubes entering their noses, and the vacuum sucks out the dark gastric acids that might build up and digest their stressed stomachs. Trauma patients often get ulcers.

Other tubes run through surgical incisions and into the chest and torso, sucking out pus and mucus from around the injured organs. The nurse uses still more tubes to evacuate saliva from the patient's mouth and yellow phlegm from his lungs. All these secretions accumulate in the Dispolex. Occasionally a Dispolex will have to be changed during the day, but the night shift has to change them all, all twelve of the things, all of them usually full. Jeff likes to have done with this job as early on his shift as he can. Having delivered the blood to Freckles, he walks briskly to cubicle one, a glassed-in isolation room.

Jeff glances briefly at the patient, a young woman who lies motionless in the bed. Her eyes stare unblinking at the ceiling. Then Jeff goes directly to the Dispolex, which is nearly brimful with chartreuse liquid. Jeff replaces it with a fresh one and, carefully holding the container at arm's length, carries it down the hallway to the "dirty" utility room and dumps it into a large vat of similarly contaminated fluids. The empty canister goes into a trash bin lined with a double layer of plastic bags.

Returning quickly to the CCRU, Jeff is about to cross the red line into cubicle two when a female voice calls, "Jeff?"

Without pausing, Jeff turns and walks toward cubicle three, where a thirty-six-year old man the nurses call Billy is rallying after a brush with septic shock. The bacteria from his perforated intestine somehow found a route into the abdominal cavity and from there to the bloodstream.

A loop of small intestine, torn on impact with a steering wheel, protrudes through an incision in his belly. There, under a bandage, it can be kept sterile. The nurse wants Jeff to help her change that bandage.

"Lemme wash my hands," Jeff says. He stands at the sink for several minutes, lathering with antiseptic soap.

Downstairs in the admitting area, the killer is blood loss. Here in the CCRU, it's infection, so a simple dressing change becomes a major project. When Jeff's hands are sufficiently clean, the nurse is waiting for him with masked face and gloved hands.

As she calls for each item, Jeff picks it up and opens its germ-proof container in such a way as to make the item protrude. There is a trick to it, but Jeff has had practice and the nurse's hands stay germfree.

When the nurse can spare him for a few minutes, Jeff himself puts on gloves and mask and attacks the smaller dressings himself. He works smoothly, but carefully, the way the trauma nurses taught him. It is a specific procedure.

Gently, Jeff removes the old dressing over the Swan-

Ganz catheter that extends through the patient's heart and into the lung. That's the one that allows the trauma nurse to monitor the rush of blood through the capillaries, providing an instant index on perfusion. The interface between man and machine fascinates Jeff's mathematical mind.

After removing the dressing, Jeff checks the entry wound for the pus that would warn of renewed infection. Finding none, he swabs the area with hydrogen peroxide, then sterile water and finally the ubiquitous foaming brown Betadine. The sterility assured, he places a small pad covered with antiseptic cream over the wound, covers that with several larger pads and anchors the bandage with tape.

When he is finished, Jeff neatly writes the date and time on the bandage. Respirator tubes, intravenous tubes and all dressings are changed at least once every twenty-four hours. CCRU patients are often so weakened that they can die of infections that Jeff's healthy immune system could shrug off without effort.

The nurse checks Jeff's work and reads the dial at the far end of the Swan-Ganz to make certain the sensing device hasn't been disturbed by the dressing change. The nurse is pleased. Jeff enjoys the opportunity to give hands-on care, and the gadgetry . . . Jeff's eyes go to the mathematically elegant curve that moves across the monitor screen. In the trauma unit, it is sometimes difficult to tell where the people end and the numbers begin.

In most medical institutions, an orderly with a degree in mathematics might be an oddity, but Jeff is comfortable here. Economic factors force many medical institutions to hire functional illiterates to fill the orderly jobs, but at Shocktrauma, college students and even one retired rear admiral have competed for the privilege of emptying bedpans.

The dressing change completed, Jeff proceeds back to Dispolex number two. But as he stoops to grasp the repugnant container he is interrupted by a single word.

"Jeff?"

Jeff straightens up. "Lemme wash my hands," he says to the nurse in cubicle one, glancing at the quiet woman on the bed.

The young woman is in the Shocktrauma isolation room for a number of reasons, but the fundamental one is her fear of hypodermic needles. She didn't get a tetanus shot, and that was a mistake.

The tack that penetrated her shoe was a small one, and she pulled it out and threw it away without thinking much about it. But the wound was entered by a specimen of the bacteria *Clostridium tetani*. The bacteria is common in the soil and usually doesn't live in human flesh, but sometimes it catches hold and flourishes and this was one of those times. The woman woke up one morning two weeks later and couldn't open her mouth—lockjaw.

Once, the disease was uniformly fatal. The facial muscles would draw up as the bacterial toxins poisoned the nervous system, producing a sardonic smile. The convulsions, touched off by lights or sounds, would often break bones. It was a difficult way to die, since the victim commonly retained consciousness until respiratory failure at the very end.

Modern techniques allow doctors to save most tetanus patients by the simple expedient of turning off the peripheral nervous system . . . the nerves that tell the muscles to shake and lock. After a while, if the doctors are sophisticated enough to keep the patient alive for a week or two, the immune system kills the *C. tetani*. The thing that medicine hasn't changed is that the victim still remains conscious throughout the entire ordeal. The chemical that the doctors use to stun the peripheral nervous system does not affect the neurons of the brain.

Now the nurse who cares for the paralyzed woman wants Jeff to help turn her. Like most trauma patients, her position must be shifted every two hours. The weight of her body against the soft bed squeezes the blood out of her capillaries at the point of contact. If the perfusion of the skin is compromised for more than two hours, it goes into shock and dies, and a bed sore forms. Bacteria, gaining access through the bedsore, can then invade the blood.

Turning also keeps blood from pooling into the legs and gut, starving the brain and increasing the likelihood that deadly blood clots will form and break away into the bloodstream. Regular turning also helps keep the lung fluids loose so the nurse can suck them out with a long suction tube, which reaches into the chest through the respirator fitting and, ultimately, drains into the Dispolex. Turning is essential, and one of the reasons bedsores are rare at Shocktrauma is Jeff.

The nurse waits impatiently while he washes his hands. The patient's half-open eyes stare at the ceiling.

It is an awkward job, clumsy because of the dangling lines and the extended respirator arm. The right leg goes over the left, with a pillow placed between. The patient is moved onto her left side and propped in place by a bolster of rolled towels against her back. Now the pupils stare through the bars of the railing at a crayon picture drawn by her four-year-old son.

As he departs, Jeff pauses a moment to watch the nurse drop artificial tears into the woman's eyes. There is no way to tell what a mind afraid of needles thinks about while lying paralyzed in cubicle one. Jeff always gets his tetanus shot.

Now Jeff has time to empty the cubicle two Dispolex and then, number three. He is approaching bed four when he hears it again.

"Jeff! Can you help me a minute?"

In cubicle five, Jeff lathers his hands thoroughly. The bed behind him is occupied by a man who, at the moment, is the unit's most precarious customer. The twenty-five-year-old electrician was helping rebuild an inner-city row house when a brick wall collapsed on him.

The falling bricks cracked his skull, broke both legs in several places, smashed his right kneecap and snapped every rib in his chest. The ambulance medic recognized the textbook flail chest immediately. Every time the man's diaphragm moved, the entire front of his chest collapsed. The man is alive because the ambulance medic drove past two local hospitals and was met at the dumpster by an admitting nurse and anesthesiologist.

The principal function of the rib cage is to hold the chest wall firm so the diaphragm's downward movement can create a vacuum that draws air into the lungs. In a flail chest patient, the sucking collapses the chest instead

124

of expanding the lungs. Unless the lungs are inflated from the outside, the patient suffocates.

The ambulance medic started pumping air into the electrician's lungs even before the rescue squad had him freed from the rubble, and the admitting team attached an Engstrom as soon as he arrived. Admitting team surgeons pushed large hollow tubes between his second and third ribs on both sides to drain the air and blood that were already accumulating inside the battered chest cavity. Then, for hours, orthopedic surgeons worked to install stainless steel pins through his fractured arms and legs. Miraculously, there was no abdominal bleeding.

For forty-eight hours the patient failed to improve, but he didn't get any worse and that is a good sign in the CCRU. But two hours ago a routine blood study reported that the oxygen content in his blood was beginning to drop. The respirator settings were changed to pump more oxygen into the lungs, but the blood gases haven't improved, so the lungs are probably filling with fluid. That's a treatable condition, but first an X ray is needed to rule out other problems and identify which parts of the lungs are clogging up. That's where Jeff comes in. Jeff helps lift the patient, gently, gently, gently, while the nurse slides the X-ray plate between him and the bed.

Quickly, while the X-ray technician is shooting, Jeff runs to change the Dispolex in the electrician's cubicle and returns in time to wash his hands again and help with the removal of the photographic plate.

That done, he heads toward the Dispolex in cubicle four, but he slips on a small puddle of Betadine. He regains his balance and changes direction. Up on the island, he tells the clerk to call housekeeping to mop up the antiseptic. Shocktrauma orderlies are far too valuable to spend their time cleaning floors.

"Jeff? Has anyone seen Jeff? Oh, JEFF . . . "

Like orderlies everywhere, Jeff's job is to take care of small things. His unusual status results from the fact that, in trauma medicine, it's the small things that kill the patient, the small things that the nurses might forget to correct if they had to empty bedpans and fuss with the Dispolexes.

Ultimately, the difference is Cowley, who did his share of dirty work and has a profound respect for honest labor. His perspective on this matter makes him an eccentric among Baltimore doctors.

Baltimore is a medical town that has produced surgeons like Halstead and Blalock, internists like Osler, opthalmologists like Wilmer and pediatricians like Taussig. Biologists from Baltimore figured heavily in the conquest of polio. Bufferin comes from Baltimore and the increasingly popular "belly-button" sterilization procedure for women was developed there as well. Medicine, like steel, is one of Baltimore's principal exports and its practice is viewed locally with a reverence approaching awe. When the medical society petitions the state legislature for favors, the legislature complies respectfully. The doctors of Baltimore are generally the offspring of the affluent and they form one of the last genuine aristocracies. It is not strictly necessary to ride to hounds, or sail on the Chesapeake Bay, but many do. Baltimore doctors are first, last and always gentlemen.

Cowley, on the other hand, paid his dues in full. He worked his way through college and medical school while struggling to support a family. He washed cars, drove trucks, and eventually landed a job pushing wheelbarrows full of concrete under the hot Utah sun during the construction of Hill Air Force Base. The foreman was intrigued with Cowley's hard work and quixotic dream of becoming a doctor, so when the opportunity arose, he offered the young man a promotion to a job that might allow a little time to study. Cowley became the night janitor in a large barracks-like building used during the day as a sweatshop for draftsmen designing the base's facilities.

For Jeff, the worst of it is the Dispolexes. For Cowley, it was the spitoons.

"The spitoons... every one of the draftsmen had one, big brass ones, and there'd be spit and snot and tobacco all over the things. I'd have to load 'em up and take 'em down to the latrine and clean them out and polish them, and that was *bad*. I didn't mind the other stuff but Jeez, I used to get so sick. You had to get down and chip this stuff off with your fingernails. I always wanted to go in and tell those guys, Jesus Christ, either miss it or spit in it, but don't leave the snot just hanging down... you know how cuspidors are... I hated it."

But he did it, and he earned his degree, and he went to medical school in faraway Baltimore.

It was a hard life for Cowley and his family, but it taught him lessons that few doctors learn, lessons that his Mormon upbringing in Layton, Utah, had primed him to understand. "We were always taught at home," he remembers, slipping into his country boy persona, "the the guy who dug the hole for the shithouse could be just as much of a perfectionist as anybody. It was an honest dollar and the idea was to do the job well. There was no stigma attached. There was no stigma attached to any job, if you did it well."

Cowley's meticulous concern with low-echelon efficiency was the foundation of his success with the death laboratory, and now it frequently translates into adulation from the nurses, attendants and housekeeping people. But it does not fit the standard operating procedures of the medical community and it drives administrators to distraction.

John Ashworth, who administers the multi-million dollar Shocktrauma budget and tries vainly to hold Cowley's nose to the bureaucratic grindstone, grouses at length. He complains principally about Cowley's tendency to meddle in affairs he does not comprehend. Like garbage bags.

"They ran out of them upstairs," Ashworth says in shell-shocked exasperation. "So a nurse went to get a trash can and it didn't have a garbage bag in it."

In Ashworth's view of the universe, such petty slip-ups are inevitable in large hospitals. They have to be taken in stride, with a little bellyaching to let off steam.

But today, while Ashworth was preparing to discuss a little matter of eight-and-a-half-million dollars with Cowley, the nurse looked down into the trash can and saw that there was no garbage bag liner inside. Trash cans without liners are an infection hazard. The nurse blew her stack. At about that time, Cowley walked by on his way to the meeting with Ashworth and the nurse grabbed him by the sleeve of his lab coat.

"They know they can do that and he'll listen," Ashworth says. "And he'll make it into a really big, serious incident. He'll talk to you in this real quiet voice and say, 'Well, why can't you get garbage bags?' He'll go through the whole process, assess the whole problem and then bring it to me. He gets pissed off when I try to explain it to him. He can't understand why there can't be a simple system derived for getting garbage bags."

Ashworth slumps deeper into his chair. He is the man in charge of logistics. He's supposed to see that the meals get cooked, the supplies get ordered, the bills get paid, the cleanup gets done, the requisitions get honored, the budgets get prepared and the payrolls get met. Hospital administrators have clout.

When Ashworth became the Shocktrauma administrator years ago he never expected to stay so long. But he, too, fell victim to the Cowley charisma, and he stays. But his admiration for Cowley's dream doesn't blunt his frustration with the Cowley approach to management.

By the time Cowley finished discussing the garbage bag problem with Ashworth, he had important medical matters to attend to, he was late and the eight-and-a-half-million-dollar budget problem went undiscussed. The financial paperwork now lies in a file basket while Ashworth ponders his marching orders with distaste. His instructions are to make one specific person responsible for garbage bags.

So it is that Ashworth has his albatross, but the nurses

have their garbage bags, and Jeff doesn't mop floors. Jeff?

"Jeff! Jeff? Is Jeff anywhere around?"

There is a respirator with a hair-trigger alarm by bed twelve. The alarm goes off continually, but everything is fine. The nurse has checked, and checked and triple-checked, and still the alarm sounds at ten-minute intervals. At first it was an irritant, then a hassle. Finally, the malfunctioning alarm triggered itself just as the nurse was about to inject a syringe of blood into a test tube. Turning her head automatically toward the patient, she injected her finger instead.

The nurse is furious. Protocol now requires her to report the incident to the disease control officer and to get a fresh tetanus shot. She is mad enough to throw the test tube into the garbage can, and that is too mad to touch the respirator safely. Would Jeff look at the miserable goddamned thing?

Fifteen minutes later, Jeff wraps a piece of electrician's plastic tape around a bare wire and disappears toward the Dispolex canisters in cubicles number six and seven. He tucks one full container under each arm and heads toward the dirty room, but the mention of his name stops him as he passes beneath the clerk's station on the island. The admitting nurse downstairs and the clerk on the island are trying to figure out how to put together enough people to take a head case to CATscan while at the same time preparing to bring the stellate fracture upstairs.

"Why don't we just send Jeff to CATscan to pick her up when she's finished?" the clerk is offering. "Would that work?"

130

"That's a solution," says the intercom. "We'll do that."

Jeff, still holding the two Dispolexes of reddish-brown fluid, opens his mouth to protest, but a word from behind the island cuts him short.

"Jeff?"

"Can it wait a minute?" Jeff answers, heading for the dirty room with the Dispolexes. "I'm coming, I'm coming."

17

CHRISTINE? THE NURSE TRAINEE ASKS. THE FLOW of blood from Christine's ear has stopped now and the rivulet is solidifying.

The patient lies still on the metal scanner tray, a respirator clicking rhythmically beside her, her head positioned to slide easily, when the time comes, into the center hole of the large steel donut that fills a quarter of the room. The Computerized Axial Tomography (CAT) scanner is the most sophisticated, and the most expensive, diagnostic tool of modern medical science.

As she stands by the donut and keeps an eye on Christine, the nurse trainee can see the CATscan operator through a thick lead-glass window. The woman is pushing buttons with a manicured finger and her face is distorted by an aggravated scowl. Again, the nurse trainee bends over Christine and pronounces her name.

An unexpected noise from behind her makes her turn quickly to find the neurosurgeon looking down at her from behind his beard. "She can't hear you, you know," the man says.

"You don't know that," the trainee replies.

The neurosurgeon shrugs. "Whatever you say." He displays the wan smile that is the stock defense mechanism of the brain surgery business. He walks back to the control room, absently slapping the rubber end of his reflex hammer against the palm of his left hand. The trainee watches him whisper something in the operator's ear.

Beyond the glass, the scanner operator answers without taking her eyes away from the flashing panel before her. "I'll need some time to think about it," she says with exaggerated thoughtfulness. "I've never done it in a broom closet before."

Obviously pleased with himself, the neurosurgeon squeezes behind an admitting room nurse who accompanied Christine to CATscan and now talks on the telephone. She is using a ballpoint pen to write notes on the hem of her pink scrub dress. The neurosurgeon proceeds back, out of the operation area and into a small conference area. He sits down in a plastic chair, leans back and fishes around in the wastebasket for a handful of random CATscan photos. Idly, he shuffles through the Polaroid prints.

In the center of each print, there is the oval representation of the human skull, what the technicians call a slice, taken horizontally at eyebrow and eartop level. The gray matter in the oval is, realistically enough, gray.

The neurosurgeon examines the first Polaroid. The brain tumor is a clear black mass on the left side, which probably means that the right side of the victim's body is paralyzed. Inoperable. The neurosurgeon tosses the print back into the wastebasket.

The next slice shows an atrophied brain. The triangular ventricles in the center of each hemisphere, normally small cavities filled with spinal fluid, have enlarged as the brain shrank. Now the ventricles are the size of tangerines and the brain has shrunk to the thickness of a watermelon rind. Presumably, viruses are killing the brain cells. Alzheimer's Disease . . . it used to be called senility. The slice flutters to the bottom of the wastebasket.

Nearby, the admitting room nurse hangs up the telephone and returns to her patient. She tells the trainee that she just talked to Christine's next-door neighbor. While she checks the patient's intravenous lines, listens to the heart and takes a blood pressure, she recaps the conversation. Christine is an honor student and an accomplished violinist who had a scholarship to the Peabody Institute. The nurse says "had." Christine's parents are on their way to the unit.

"The guy who hit her was drunk. Some guy in a pickup truck, wasn't even hurt. It happens like that a lot."

The trainee's eyes focus on the encrusted blood on Christine's right ear. The nurse glances at her. "Look," she says, "if you're gonna stay, I'll go inside and do some paperwork."

"Sure," says the trainee, reaching out with her left hand to pick away a chip of dried blood from the earlobe.

In a few minutes the neurosurgeon, bored with the Polaroids, returns to the scan room. He stands at his patient's feet and scrapes her soles with the hammer handle. Nothing.

"It's a damn shame," he says. "She was so pretty, too."

The trainee, leaning against the wall with her arms folded, shakes her head. "Was?" she asks. "You give up easily."

"No," the surgeon says. "If I was giving up, I wouldn't be here. I'm just being realistic. She's got no blood flow to her brain . . . well, not much when I looked, probably nothing by now. If it's a clot, we can go in and relieve the pressure, but it's probably too late. It was probably too late when she came in."

"All the same," the trainee says, "you shouldn't talk like that. It makes it sound like it doesn't bother you."

The neurosurgeon looks at her. "It doesn't," he says.

The CATscan operator and the admitting nurse step out from behind the glass partition. The machine is ready, and the group carefully slides the tray forward, until the patient's head is inside the donut. Soon, Christine is alone in the room. The neurosurgeon, the nurse and the nurse trainee stand behind the CATscan operator and watch through the glass. The technician's fingers move cross the panel, touching buttons. Something hums loudly, and there is a sharp click.

"Damn," the technician says, pushing buttons again.

"The scanner is down half the time," the nurse tells the trainee. "They're full of bugs."

The trainee tells the nurse that the hospital she just left had wanted a CATscanner, but the bureaucrats wouldn't let them buy it. Too much money.

"It ain't the price," the CATscan technician mutters. "It's the upkeep."

The neurosurgeon wanders back into the conference

pit. Christine's angiogram, the one taken in Admitting, lies in a large brown envelope on the table. The man toys with the envelope for a moment, slides the film out, and holds it up to the ceiling light. To him, it speaks eloquently.

In the third collision, Christine's brain absorbed the energy of the head colliding with the side window. The energy echoed inside the skull, bouncing off the concave inner surfaces of the bone, damaging membranes and capillaries and bruising the brain cells themselves. Immediately, the swelling began. The skull was unyielding.

The pressure built quickly, mashing the blood-carrying arteries. The already-swelling cells began to suffocate, and the swelling intensified. The pressure squashed the arteries further. Again, the neurosurgeon examines the X ray. He suspects that another angiogram, done now, would show the brain totally bereft of blood supply.

Still, the CATscan **might** show something else. If the pressure is due to a **torn artery** and subsequent blood clot, rather than the generalized swelling of cells, then there is something a surgeon can do. He can drill into the skull and suck the blood clot out, relieving the pressure. The CATscan might show a clot. Or the ventricles might be shoved out of line by a mass somewhere. If any blood at all is getting into Christine's skull, she has a chance. As long as she has a chance, the trauma team will continue to fight.

Occasionally, there is a fluke. There was, for instance, Dutch Ruppersberger, an assistant state's attorney. He came directly from the scene of a head-on collision and it was one of those cases where the trauma team had to take a deep breath before going to work.

His chest crushed, bleeding profusely from the head, the patient was deep in shock. Tiny bubbles under the skin marked the places where his lungs were punctured. There was barely enough oxygen in his blood to support life, and the X ray showed a skull fracture. The monitors confirmed the ominous outlook. At many emergency rooms he would have been dead on arrival, but Shock-trauma's admitting protocols don't allow that. So they worked on him and he kept trying to die, but never did. He lived to be transferred upstairs but the general assumption was that the shock would result in fatal brain damage.

As an accident victim fights his way back to consciousness, hearing is the first of the five senses to return. Ruppersberger recovered that ability as several trauma doctors stood beside his bed, debating the question of intracranial pressures. The consensus was that the pressure in the patient's skull would soon rise high enough to cause brain death.

Some people refer to Ruppersberger's subsequent recovery as a miracle, but the neurosurgeon waiting in the CATscan pit knows better. Not a miracle, a fluke. Neurosurgeons often give powerful drugs called corticosteroids to combat brain swelling, but it is usually too late. Steroids are also prescribed for asthma, and Ruppersberger, an asthmatic, had been taking heavy doses before his accident. Some lives are charmed.

The neurosurgeon looks at Christine's X ray again. He'll give her the best shot he can. He can't do any better. He wasn't driving the pickup.

"SHOOTING," the technician warns. Beyond the leaded glass the heavy steel donut rotates an inch, whining loudly. With a thunk, it stops. Again it moves and stops, moves and stops, and then a red light flashes at the technician.

"Damn," she says, slamming a manual down on the counter.

The neurosurgeon will deal with the facts. The scanner will give him the facts. If he quarreled with facts, he'd never make it as a neurosurgeon.

The trauma unit's record on brain trauma is impressive. Good hospitals work hard to save one out of every three serious head trauma cases, but Shocktrauma saves two out of three. The neurosurgeon is acutely aware that the success rate has little to do with fancy brain surgery, though. It has to do with controlling shock. If the admitting team can hold the shock at bay, the brain cells won't suffocate and they won't be injured by poisons in the bloodstream.

But when the swelling is rapid and massive . . . the skull is a tight box. One by one, the vital functions switch off.

"SHOOTING . . . never mind."

If the CATscan will show him a clot, he can remove it.

"SHOOTING!"

The donut hums and rolls, hums and rolls, hums and rolls. The technician examines her fingernails and grins. The donut hums and rolls.

The neurosurgeon is standing in front of the screen when the image appears. The two hemispheres of the brain are clearly visible, and in the center of each hemisphere there is a thin opening. The ventricles are squeezed almost closed. The swelling is irreversible.

"That's what I figured," the neurosurgeon says to the trainee beside him.

"Aren't you proud of yourself?" she snaps, turning away. The neurosurgeon watches her as she walks out the door, then turns back to the screen, where another slice a half-inch higher, appears. Data. No good doctor ever quarrels with data.

18

———

SOMEWHERE THERE IS A CHECKLIST, BUT FRECK-
les doesn't need it.

She stands for a moment in the middle of cubicle
nine, where the bed will soon be, and her eyes run
across the cabinets. In the right corner of the cubicle
the respirator hose quivers each time the Engstrom
puffs a breath of air into the room. An electrocardiograph cable lies coiled in its proper place and the main
vacuum line sucks air into the Dispolex with a slight
hiss. The lights on the electronic equipment are all on.
Intravenous bottles, tape, gloves, catheters, gauze,
pressure tubing, hypodermic needles, rectal probe.
Freckles had checked all these things earlier, and now
she checks her mind to make sure she checked everything.

Behind her, the boy's bed moves out from behind
the island, slowly, slowly. The patient's form is shielded
from view by the team of gowned doctors, nurses and
attendants. Travel along the edge of death is a delicate
affair.

The anesthesiologist walks behind the bed, bending over Larry's head. The Engstrom was disconnected in the operating room, and now the Bengali bags his patient, inflating the lungs from a black rubber bag that he squeezes rhythmically. The black bag is connected by a hose to a green steel cylinder that rides in a cradle under the rolling bed. A nurse fusses with the valve on one of the bags that sway over the bed. Tex walks alongside with his fingers wrapped around the boy's right wrist. The pulse is weak, but regular.

At the mouth of the cubicle the bed is turned around and steered head-first toward the far wall. Freckles reaches around the anesthesiologist and clips the Engstrom's hose over the large plastic orifice that protrudes from the windpipe at the base of the patient's neck.

The nurse's fingers automatically touch the valves and switches, making adjustments, testing instrumentation, running down the memorized checklist. Quietly the respirator fills and then empties the lungs, pumping a warm, moist mixture of oxygen and sterile air. Three dots move steadily across the monitor screen high on the wall. The top dot bounces crazily as the nurse sticks an electrocardiograph sensor onto the boy's chest, near the right shoulder. Soon the top dot bounces steadily, 80 beats a minute, still a little shocky.

When all the leads are in place, the three dots bounce in syncopation. The top one leaps when nerves to the heart issue the electrical command to beat. The second one measures pressures inside the heart and jumps when the actual contraction occurs. The third dot rises a fraction of a second later, when the arteries swell under the pressure of the ejected blood.

Frequently, as she pauses by the bedside, Freckles rests one hand on the patient. As she peers at the bank of gauges, her right hand automatically pats the boy's shoulder, touches his lifeless fingers. Larry lies still, the lashes of his half-closed eyes wet with artificial tears.

A clutter of bags and bottles hangs above the bed, each with a dangling plastic tube. Some of the tubes intersect in hard plastic Y fittings with tiny thumbwheel valves. Other tubes run directly into the veins.

The heart signal momentarily jumps off the screen as the nurse shakes several of the lines to untangle them. Later she will replace all the tubing in a systematic fashion, but for now it is enough for her to know where everything is, in case of emergency. The lines untangled, she wraps a blood pressure cuff around the right bicep and compares the reading with the numbers on the electronic monitor. They match. She repeats the cross-check with temperature, pulse and respiration functions.

The various readings, analyzed in combination, tell Freckles everything she needs to know about Larry's ability to perfuse himself. Dial swings and changing numbers will warn her when his heart tires, when internal bleeding begins, when his arteries become exhausted and relax. The preservation of life is the long-range goal, but the medical battle itself swirls around the sometimes routine, sometimes desperate need to maintain the vital numbers. Numbers. Numbers and chemistry.

Now that Larry has survived the accident, the helicopter ride, the operating room and the trip upstairs, it is necessary for the trauma team to pause and reassess the situation. For that, they need numbers. Blood rushes through a hollow needle and into a syringe. Freckles squirts the fresh blood into three test tubes.

"These need to go downstairs, stat," she says to Jeff, handing him the samples. He disappears.

"Stat" means immediately. It's an old piece of medical jargon that became the first cliché of trauma medicine. It means that Jeff walks downstairs to the third floor lab instead of waiting for the elevator. It means a flurry of activity in what the trauma team has come to call the stat lab. In minutes, a mechanical pencil located on the CCRU island scrawls out a series of numbers. They are not the values the traumatologists would like to see, but they will do. Comfortable.

Since the bleeding was stopped in the operation room, Larry's blood, aided by blood bank clotting components, has almost regained the ability to coagulate normally. The level of oxygen-carrying hemoglobin molecules in the blood is high enough to support life safely. But the readings are a little acidic and the electrolytes are slightly awry. Freckles will have to watch that.

Aeons ago, life on earth consisted of single cells suspended in the primordial sea. They took their nourishment directly from the surrounding waters and excreted their waste products to be carried away, automatically, by the currents.

As more complicated animals evolved, the sea became private and internal in the form of blood, but it retained the original salts and the chemically-useful pH, or acid-alkaline balance, of roughly neutral. When the first creatures slithered onto land, they took that inner sea with them.

The balances have changed slightly in the millions of years since then, but the individual cells of the human body are as dependent on the blood's constancy as the first cells were on the never-changing sea.

Shock destroys the fragile chemical make-up of the blood. For instance, cells that are short of oxygen respond like an automobile engine with a faulty carburetor. They spew out acid exhaust, and in the case of the trauma patient, the corrosive waste products can turn the blood sour.

The heart muscle, which is especially sensitive to changes in blood chemistry, responds to the rising acid levels by ceasing to beat.

The salts are also critical. The balance between potassium and sodium salts regulates the rhythm of Larry's heart, and if the proportions oscillate too wildly, the heart will begin to beat erratically and then, again, stop.

The kidneys normally function to rid the blood of too much potassium, a side effect of multiple blood transfusions. When the kidneys cease to function, potassium levels can rise quickly until the heart begins twitching uncontrollably. In that scenario, too, the heart eventually stops.

Doctors have long known that swings in blood chemistry can lead to cardiac arrest and death. One of Cowley's most important contributions to medicine was his discovery that even minor oscillations in blood chemistry can lead to secondary shock and a slower demise.

Freckles's attempts to maintain Larry's salt balances and blood acid levels are complicated by his metabolism's own mindless attempts to fight for life. Within seconds of his accident, the sudden drop in blood pressure triggered the well-known fight-or-flight mechanism and powerful chemicals were released into his bloodstream.

The rush of adrenaline and other hormones triggered a set of chemical reactions that resulted in a sudden change in the normal pattern of blood flow. The arteries that led to his skin, gut, kidneys and liver clamped down, hard. Simultaneously, vessels leading to the brain opened up and blood rushed to his head.

When the fight-or-flight mechanism is provoked by fear, the mind races. Survivors of highway crashes report that time slows and the procession of events, the color of the oncoming car, the details of the guard rail, the shrieks of terror, all imprint themselves forever on the whirring brain. Then comes the crash, the bleeding and the unconsciousness that follows a sudden drop in blood pressure.

The metabolic response to injury evolved to help primitive man think fast in emergencies and, with luck, avoid injury. Without luck, given a relatively minor wound to the skin and muscle, the reduced blood flow to those areas would temper the bleeding and allow the victim to crawl back into the bushes before passing out. Eventually, if the blood loss is minor enough, he might recover with an intact brain.

The body's damage control system wasn't designed for multiple trauma. In ancient times, badly injured people simply died, as they often die today.

When Cowley began saving accident victims from the immediate effects of shock, he discovered that the powerful biochemicals didn't shut off just because the doctor had arrived. And the continuous high levels of the fight-or-flight substances could and did kill vital organs.

While it is true that the preferential blood flow to the brain makes sense in the short term, the strategy is only useful for about an hour. By that time, the liver and kidneys have begun to suffocate and the patient may ultimately die regardless of the condition of his brain.

Nature, in short, did not anticipate Freckles.

She stoops at the foot of the bed to examine the urine bag. It is almost empty. The kidney cells aren't working, but with luck they're not dead and, with proper care, will recover. If they don't, Maryland has a kidney dialysis program.

In the meantime, Freckles will fight the potassium buildup. The fluids that flow downward into Larry's veins are deliberately devoid of potassium, and later the nurse may have to administer enemas of a special liquid that will suck potassium out of the blood vessels of the large intestine. A portable dialysis machine waits in the nephrology wing of the hospital for Freckles's call.

The nurse rises from the foot of the bed and stands over the boy. His heartbeat seems to have speeded slightly, just a little. The numbers confirm her senses. Leaning between two streams of descending plastic tubes, she strokes Larry's head with her left hand.

"Larry? Can you hear me Larry? You had an accident and we're taking care of you. You're in the hospital, Larry." Larry doesn't respond. His eyelids are open slightly and the nurse closes them gently with her fingers. Maybe he hears, probably he doesn't. For now, his body fights as best it can.

Every individual in the colony of cells has been to some degree damaged by shock. Membranes must be repaired, enzyme stockpiles must be rebuilt, the dead and dying cells must be disassembled and disposed of.

Tomorrow, the nurse will start dripping high-caloric protein and sugar compounds into Larry's veins. At a thousand calories per liter of liquid, the trauma team may be able to send three thousand calories a day into the boy's body before it begins to react dangerously to the volume of liquid. Three thousand calories a day may not be enough, but it will help. A healing trauma patient can starve to death while getting enough calories to make a healthy ditchdigger fat.

Starvation, like fluctuating salt and clotting factor levels, is a secondary complication of shock. One of the Baltimore trauma unit's principal contributions to medicine was the discovery that oscillating chemical balances were the most common cause of death in post-shock patients. The critical corollary was that those oscillations could be controlled.

The changing function of the kidneys, heart and other obvious organs are relatively simple to monitor, but the diffuse biochemical organizations like the immune system are poorly understood. So are the critical biofeedback mechanisms upon which the metabolism depends.

One of the better-known such mechanisms involves the blood pressure regulatory system, a set of biological, thermostat-like switches located at strategic places in the vascular tree. Each switch is composed of a microscopic clump of cells whose duties are to sense the pressure and produce the messenger chemicals that will correct any deviations from normal. Cowley and other trauma scientists believe that shock damage to such systems composes the Achilles' heel of the CCRU patient.

Poisoned and half-suffocated, the living thermostats are sluggish, slow to sense changes in the bloodstream and even slower in applying corrective measures. And once those corrective measures have achieved the goal of normalcy, the sensor cells forget to turn them off. The result is neglect followed by overcorrection followed by neglect. Oscillations.

Freckles won't try to explain this to Larry's father when she calls him later. She will talk, instead, about one secondary effect of the oscillations: disruption of the immune system.

Freckles, like the other trauma nurses, is phobic about germs. The smell of disinfectant is strong in the cubicle and as the night proceeds the trash pail collects pair after pair of once-sterile rubber gloves.

Total sterility is an ideal, of course. Germs enter the trauma patient's wounds at the time of the accident and, even if they don't, the bowel is crawling with bacteria. The nurses hope the patient's own immune system, plus the antibiotics, can control those microbes while the nurse, for her part, scrupulously avoids adding to the problem. The unit's survival rate indicates that her efforts are usually successful. Usually, but not always.

Sometimes, despite the efforts, the patient spikes a fever and won't respond to the antibiotics. The fever rises and falls, rises and falls, and the nurse tries to remember if she did anything wrong a day or two days

148

before. Too often a young person is rescued from death at the roadside, brought back to life in the admitting area and nursed through eight days in the CCRU only to die of a common infection. At such times, even a trauma nurse is susceptible to tears.

With Larry checked in and stable, Freckles disappears into the next cubicle to check a few dials and make an entry in Walter's record.

"How you doin', Walter?" she asks as she examines the electronics.

"Hurtin', mama."

"I'll give you something in a minute, OK?"

Back in cubicle nine, Freckles pauses to catalog the things she's done and those she still has to do. The plastic suction tube that the surgeons left imbedded in Larry's right chest is draining bloody fluid into a graduated plastic trap and, on the television screen, the three dots bounce in textbook fashion. Lights flicker on the blue electronic box that pumps red blood cells into the boy's arms at a predetermined, metered rate. Larry hasn't moved.

Freckles will change the intravenous tubes. They were exposed to the unsterile air in the elevator and the hallways, and they make her nervous. Then she'll bathe and shampoo him with antiseptic soap. And the linens. Freckles will feel more comfortable if they are clean, sterile ones.

As she works steadily, the electronic womb that Cowley built monitors Larry's metabolism and blood chemistry. As necessary, the nurse makes minor course corrections, adding clotting factor during the middle of her shift and, an hour before dawn, a blood thinner.

Methodically, Freckles changes the dressings that cover each tube's penetration point. She touches the boy and talks softly to him. Long before scientists proved the fact, nurses understood that touching improves survival rate. Soon, she tells her apparently unconscious charge, she will talk to his parents.

19

WHEN THE ELEVATOR DOORS OPEN, TEX CAN HEAR
the woman screaming, "My face, my face, oh, God, my
face." The surgeon closes his eyes and lets his breath
escape between his teeth. The clock says 4:55. Tex
hasn't been to bed, his feet hurt and his stomach is full
of stale coffee. And now, a screamer.

"Do you know who my husband is?" the woman
shrieks as the stretcher rolls by Tex. The admitting
nurse says the patient is breathing okay, has a rapid
pulse but no external bleeding to speak of except her
face. Some lacerations there, but not as bad as she
makes them sound. But she's got a steering wheel mark
on her belly, and her screams intensify when the bruise
is touched.

"Her name is Mary," the nurse says. "She's married
to some banker who lives out in the Valley. Also, she
smells like a Baltimore Street bar."

The helicopter medic, shoulder holster strapped over
his brown flight suit, comes in through the stairway

151

doors. He needs two of his folding stretchers back, and the admitting nurse points to them.

"Watch this one," the medic says, nodding toward Mary. "She tried to bite me. She's lucky she didn't. She's in enough trouble after what she did to her husband's Porsche. Damn, that was a pretty car. Sort of silver-colored . . . "

"HEY!" the anesthesiologist shouts. "I need some help over here."

The admitting nurse whirls in time to see Mary struggling to sit up on the table. A tall metal stand rocks precariously and there is the sound of shattered glass.

"Let me up, you raghead son of a bitch," Mary screams. "Do you know who my husband is?"

Tex looks at the helicopter medic. "How bad did she hurt the Porsche?" he asks. The medic nods, sadly. Bad. Total loss. Tex turns his attention to the struggle in Admitting one.

A medical student is holding one of the patient's arms and an attendant has the other. The fingernails bite savagely into the attendant's forearm, and he grits his teeth and hangs on.

The admitting nurse, one hand on each shoulder, slowly forces her down. The nurse's face is close to Mary's, and their eyes are locked. "Quiet down now," the nurse says, gently. "Easy now, you're just making it harder on yourself."

The admitting nurse remains in place, holding down on the shoulders, keeping eye contact. A surgical resident takes advantage of the situation and moves in, scrubbing the woman's groin with Betadine. Mary bucks and struggles at the contact.

152

"Get your hands off me," she shouts. "Get your hands off me!"

"Mary, Mary, be nice now," the admitting nurse counsels.

In the meantime the medical student has tied a rope of thick gauze around one of Mary's wrists and secured it to the table. On the other side the attendant has done the same. Tex stands at the foot of the bed.

With his left hand, the resident finds the femoral artery. Concentrating, he lowers the needle to the skin.

"You're going to feel a little stick now, Mary," the surgeon says. The needle slides deep into the tissue. Mary shrieks.

"Somebody get her legs," the resident commands. Tex grabs one ankle and a nurse holds the other.

"Mary, stop that," the admitting nurse snaps, her face close to the patient's. Mary looks at her fiercely, hatred showing. Without warning, she spits in the nurse's face.

The nurse holds her position, but her eyes grow cold. "You shouldn't have done that," the attendant says, under his breath. The hard eyes stay fixed on the patient's, and the patient tries to turn away, and fails. She looks back at the nurse and, suddenly, begins to cry.

The nurse stands up. Taking a large pad of gauze, she wipes the spittle from her face.

"At least give me something for the pain," Mary cries. "Please."

The anesthesiologist tries to explain that he's afraid to give her any drugs until he knows what's wrong with her. "I wanna go to sleep," Mary cries, not listening, shaking her head from side to side. "Ow, ow, ow, ow, ow," she sobs, "Are you gonna stick me any more?"

"Many times," says the admitting nurse, turning away.

Tex, still standing at the foot of the bed, asks Mary where she hurts. She says he should fix her face. Instead of replying, Tex walks over to her right side, puts two fingers into her tied-down right hand and tells her to squeeze.

"It hurts," says Mary. "Please, it hurts. Give me something."

"Mary," Tex orders, "squeeze my fingers." The hand closes around his fingers.

Tex leans over her chest, feeling for broken ribs. Suddenly he stops, cocking his head. Frowning, he stands.

"Mary?" he says. "Does your chest hurt?"

"My face hurts," she says.

Tex looks at the gashed cheek, then back to her chest. Finally he goes to her abdomen, probing gently with two fingers.

"Ow, ow, stop it! That hurts!"

Tex presses again, experimentally, several times. Mary shrieks louder every time. "Will somebody please call my husband," she begs. "I want to talk to my husband."

Tex changes position, so he can stand above the patient's face. "Mary?" he says.

"What do you want?" Mary replies, turning her face away.

"Mary, we're doing laboratory studies. We don't

have the results back yet, but I'm afraid you may have some internal injuries."

"What does that mean?" she asks, apprehensively.

"That means I'm going to have to make a tiny incision just above your navel. It's a small surgical procedure, but we have to do it. We have to know if you're bleeding inside."

"But it hurts!" Mary cries.

"I know, Mary," says Tex, gently, trying to console her with his voice. "Just hang in there a little longer."

"I can't, I can't, I can't. Why don't you just leave me alone?" Tex studies her face, then walks away.

Already the surgical resident and the student are laying out the belly pack and arranging the sterile drape. Tex pulls on his rubber gloves and begins to swab the belly. The nurse hands him a hypodermic syringe full of Novocaine. "You're going to feel a little prick now," he says to Mary. The needle pierces the flesh.

"You son of a bitch!" Mary screams. "If you cut me I'll sue you."

Tex stops instantly. He looks at the admitting nurse. "Has anybody called this lady's husband?" he says.

"Nobody knows where he is," the nurse answers.

"Mary," says Tex, standing up. "Do you know where your husband is?"

"The son of a bitch is supposed to be home," Mary snaps.

Tex drops the Novocaine syringe loudly onto the belly tray, snaps his gloves into the trash can and walks out of the admitting area. The nurse follows him out. Mary lunges against her arm restraints and the anesthesiologist reaches for a vial of Valium.

Outside, Tex talks to the nurse. How much does she know about the accident?

"I think she hit a tree, pretty hard. The trooper seemed kind of sheepish about bringing her, but she was unconscious when they got there. She woke up in the helicopter, which is when she tried to bite the medic. Did you see what she did to me?"

"Yeah, I saw," says Tex. "I take it she can afford lawyers?"

"I guess," the nurse says.

"Did you get a look at her right boob?"

The nurse's face instantly turns cold. "You're as bad as she is."

"No," says Tex. "I mean it. Seriously. Her right boob is smaller than her left one. Go look. You can't help but notice."

"You mean *you* couldn't help but notice."

"No," the surgeon says. "I . . . aw, Jesus, you don't think I'm . . . "

The nurse continues to stare.

"Ah, to hell with it," Tex says. "Look. Go call SYS-COM. Do it where she can't hear you. See if they can find her old man. We gotta do that belly tap."

The nurse turns coldly away.

Tex walks back to the foot of the bed and looks at his patient, who is no longer screaming. Now she's moaning softly. Tex wonders, is she quieter because of the Valium or because unseen bleeding is dulling her senses? The surgeon reviews the test results.

Her blood-alcohol level is worth whistling at, but the hematocrit came back significantly below normal. She's losing blood somewhere. Tex walks again to the head of the bed.

"Mary? Can you hear me?"

This time Mary turns toward the voice. "I can hear," she replies. The voice is hoarse from the screaming.

"Mary, the lab tests are back and they confirm that you may have some internal bleeding. I want your permission to do the procedure I told you about earlier."

"No."

"Mary, do you know what will happen to you if you are bleeding inside and we don't find it?"

"Go away."

"You'll die, Mary. If you have internal bleeding and we don't stop it, you're going to die. And it will hurt for a long time before you die."

"I want something for the pain. Give me a shot for the pain."

"We've already given you all we can. We'll give you more later, but right now we need your permission to do the belly tap."

Mary doesn't reply.

"Mary?"

"I won't really die, will I?" Mary whispers.

"You might. There's a good chance."

Mary begins to cry.

"Mary, I'm going to do the procedure. I'm going to do the belly tap. Is that okay?"

Mary cries.

"Mary, if you don't tell me it's okay, I'm not going to do it."

"No! No!"

"Fine," Tex signs. "If that's the way you want it." He turns to walk away.

"No, wait," Mary says. "I don't want to die."

"That's up to you," Tex says.

Mary suddenly looks very sober. "All right," she says, clearly. "Go ahead."

Tex wiggles his fingers into a new set of rubber gloves while the resident begins swirling Betadine over Mary's abdomen again.

"Ow, ow, ow, it hurts," Mary cries.

"I haven't done anything, yet," Tex says.

The admitting nurse returns. "There's still nobody home," she says. "No answer."

"It doesn't matter," Tex says. "The lady here decided that she didn't want to die after all."

The admitting nurse goes to the metal table, opens a metal patient's record folder and scribbles a long note. Mary cries out as the Novocaine needle darts deftly around beneath her skin. But a moment later, when the scalpel cuts, she fails to notice.

Tex stitches the tube in place and the saline flows downward, rapidly. When the bottle is placed on the floor the liquid runs back again, but now it is bright pink. When the jar is half filled, the team leader walks back to the patient's head. The admitting nurse stands at the other shoulder, adjusting the flow from a blood bag. That finished, her eyes scan the hanging bottles, move across Mary's face and down onto her chest. There, the wandering gaze stops.

"'Can you give me a shot for the pain?" Mary asks Tex.

"We're going to do better than that," Tex says. "We can put you to sleep now."

"Oh, thank God."

"I'm afraid," Tex says, "that you have internal bleeding."

The nurse slowly lifts her eyes away from Mary's breast. She looks at Tex, a lopsided expression on her face. She looks down again, then up.

"My God," she says, her voice hushed. "You were right."

20

THE GLASSED-IN SYSCOM BOOTH DOMINATES THE
the busy intersection where the CCRU entrance way
intersects with the long hall that extends through the
intensive care step-down unit. The SYSCOM dispatcher
sits inside, scrutinizing the tattered VIP notification list.
Sometimes it takes the dispatcher a few minutes to summon the courage he needs to start waking people up at
six o'clock in the morning.

The long counter in front of the dispatcher is cluttered
with stacks of electronic equipment and telephones.
Lights twinkle along a row of multi-channel monitor
scanners and the static-bracketed, cryptic conversations
of policemen, firemen and pilots fill the room.

A light stops on a scanner. "One seventy one," a
policeman's voice says, "Beltway and Reisterstown
Road, report of a 10–50-P.I., possibly involving a motorcycle."

The dispatcher puts down the VIP list and stares at
the monitor. P.I. means personal injury. A motorcycle?

This time of the year? In this weather? Motorcycle season doesn't start for two more months.

He leans forward and flips a switch to lock the monitor on that police channel. Motorcycle accidents are almost automatically assumed to involve personal injury, and that often means business for the helicopters. The dispatcher's hand goes out, switching an incoming telephone line to his headset.

"SYSCOM," he says into the headset mike. Listening, the dispatcher reaches for a clipboard and a printed form. He uses a government-issue ballpoint pen to fill in the blanks.

Far across the Chesapeake Bay, at Peninsula General Hospital in the town of Salisbury, a premature baby struggles for breath. Its tiny lungs are too immature to produce the slick substance that coats the lung and allows oxygen to pass into the bloodstream. The resulting condition, commonly known as hyaline membrane disease, is the one that killed John F. Kennedy's last son.

That famous victim focused scientific attention on the problem and, during the 1960s, a life-saving treatment was found. It is not a therapy that a small hospital can manage, however. The infant needs to be sent to the Johns Hopkins premature baby center at City Hospital, and it would never survive the long drive from Salisbury in an ambulance.

The SYSCOM dispatcher scribbles furiously. "Yes sir," he tells the doctor. "Yes sir. Yes sir, I do. I can. I'll have to call you back with an arrival time after the helicopter's in the air."

Ten years ago the doctor would have had to call the

army and work his way up the military chain of command, begging for help, before he found someone with the authority to send an aircraft. Today he picks up a telephone, dials a toll-free number and, anytime of the day or night, he's talking to someone with lots of helicopters: the man in Cowley's communications center.

The SYSCOM dispatcher breaks the circuit with the physician and dials a memorized number. A telephone rings in a cold lonely airport hangar near Salisbury and the medic looks up from the chessboard as the pilot picks up the receiver. All night, they've kept the engine warm on helicopter four, and it starts instantly.

As the Bell Jet Ranger rises above the concrete, the pilot radios SYSCOM that he's airborne. He'll be at Peninsula General in three minutes or less. SYSCOM acknowledges and the dispatcher's index finger dials Salisbury. The doctor is standing by the phone.

That done, the dispatcher rummages around for the forgotten VIP call list. Firemen battling a small blaze in an abandoned city row house chatter from one of the monitors. On another channel there is talk of a malfunctioning signal light and a long traffic backup.

"Helicopter four, SYSCOM," says a crackling voice. "Out of service at Peninsula General."

"Okay, four," says the dispatcher, noting the time.

Then, staring at the VIP call list, he waits. Waiting is his job, mostly, waiting like a spider at the center of a web, waiting to snatch patients from whichever happens to be the nearest hospital.

On the Eastern Shore, a doctor and a nurse, bundled up in long overcoats, run beneath the rotors carrying a large plastic Isolette between them. In the Isolette, served by an oxygen supply and a heater, a wrinkled, foot-long infant lies in shock. The medic fastens the Isolette securely behind the pilot.

"Four, SYSCOM. We're en route to City Hospital, estimated arrival time 7:25."

The dispatcher acknowledges and dials Baltimore City Hospital. The scanning monitors blink and stop, blink and stop. The dispatcher waits for a doctor to come to the telephone. The radios say there is a fender-bender on the Jones Falls Expressway and an aggravated assault in the ghetto. The monitor lights skip across the instrument faces, blink and stop, blink and stop. The ambulances talk to the hospitals. The firemen talk to headquarters. The cops talk to each other.

The sound of a jet comes through the SYSCOM speaker and the dispatcher looks up sharply. He keeps close track of his birds. It's helicopter one, chasing a prison escapee with its powerful floodlights.

"All units involved in the search, helicopter one reports the subject running north out of the wooded area. Units responding acknowledge." There is glee in the radio voice.

The dispatcher grins. "Go get 'em," he cheers.

Briefly, early in the shift, the dispatcher was afraid he would have to pull the helicopter out of the chase and send him off toward Montgomery County, where a Volkswagen had rear-ended a flatbed truck. Helicopter two, which ordinarily serves the Washington suburbs, is temporarily down for maintenance. As it turned out, though, the single occupant of the Volkswagen was decapitated, and the flight wasn't necessary.

If it had been, however, the dispatcher wouldn't have

hesitated to pull rank on the state police. That was the deal. Cowley said he'd help them put together an air force, as long as he had first call on it. Cowley delivered, and now the SYSCOM dispatcher collects, frequently.

"One seventy-one, headquarters," blurts the Baltimore County Police monitor. The SYSCOM dispatcher reaches for his pen, listening intently. The beltway accident. The motorcycle?

"One seventy-one, we need a state police helicopter. . . . "

The SYSCOM dispatcher doesn't wait to hear the acknowledgment from County Police headquarters. His finger mashes down on the intercom button. Downstairs in admitting a light flashes and the intercom speaker beeps.

"Baltimore County just called for a helicopter," SYSCOM says. "Beltway and Reisterstown, possibly a motorcycle."

"In Admitting, the senior nurse looks up at the speaker. "Motorcycle?" she says. "It's too early in the year."

"I'm just relaying what the police say," the speaker answers, defensively.

"Do you have an arrival time?" the nurse asks.

"Not yet. It'll be quick if it's coming. I'll let you know."

Upstairs, in the glassed-in booth, the radio crackles. The pilot of helicopter one says he's on the way to the motorcycle accident scene.

"Okay one," the dispatcher acknowledges. "Did they get that guy you were chasing?"

164

"Ten-four," says the pilot, proudly.

The dispatcher waits. A traffic patrolman reports an accident at Northern Parkway and Falls Road. The dispatcher makes no note of the fact, assuming the victim will go to the nearest hospital. Baltimore city physicians were the last in the state to acknowledge the obsolescence of the nearest-hospital philosophy, and even now, city ambulances rarely run directly to Shocktrauma.

Today such resistance is largely limited to Baltimore City, but once it was almost universal. Among other things, the doctors refused to concede that medics were capable of making decisions and performing emergency procedures that were traditionally reserved for licensed physicians. And deciding who should go to which hospital was definitely a doctor's prerogative.

Cowley and his chief anesthesiologist, Dr. McAslan, argued that policemen, dispatchers and medics could be trained, well trained. They said the old image of the omnipotent doctor was a fantasy that was costing lives.

There was, for instance, the matter of the airways.

An airway is a large-diameter plastic tube that goes into the windpipe and allows the free passage of air into the lungs. A donut-shaped balloon at the bottom of the tube secures it in place and prevents shock patients, who often vomit, from choking to death on half-digested food.

The insertion maneuver is acknowledged to be tricky, because the big tube must be eased between the tightly-strung lips of the voice box, and a mistake can cost the patient his ability to speak. As a result, the traditional logic of medicine dictated that the endotracheal tube could only be inserted by a physician.

The trauma team acknowledged the logic of this stand. But what if the patient was choking to death beside the highway and there was no doctor nearby? Wouldn't it be better to let a medic do the insertion?

No, the medical establishment said. Sorry.

Cowley, McAslan and the medics tolerated the decision because they had no choice. But they continued to resent the implication that any doctor could exercise better judgment than any layman, no matter how well trained.

In the meantime, people continued to choke to death at the scenes of accidents. By the time they got to the unit their brains were dead, and there was nothing the admitting team could do for them.

Eventually, a solution presented itself. Browsing through the literature, Dr. McAslan discovered that an ingenious inventor had designed a different sort of airway, one that anyone . . . given a little training . . . could insert safely.

The new airway didn't extend into the trachea at all. Instead it went down the esophagus. When it was in place the medic pumped up a different kind of balloon, a round solid one that sealed the passage and blocked off the liquid in the stomach. After all, if the contents of the stomach couldn't escape, the lungs were safe from vomit. Cowley and McAslan purchased the new devices, held training sessions, and handed them out to the helicopter medics. Patients started coming into the trauma unit in better shape.

The doctors' attitudes didn't change though, and one of the grimmest anecdotes in Shocktrauma history involves a young doctor who pulled rank on a medic.

It might have been a routine mission for the helicopter pilot and his medic companion. The pilot was keeping the helicopter ready on a nearby knoll and the medic had inserted the airway and was getting ready to move the patient. Then the doctor, who'd seen the accident scene and stopped his car, shoved the medic out of the way.

The doctor was disgusted. Only physicians could properly insert airways . . . here, this medic had it all wrong.

Ignoring the policeman's protests, the doctor withdrew the airway and reinserted it, the way he had been taught in medical school, with the device in the windpipe. As the medic watched in helpless horror, the doctor pumped up the balloon. Soon, the patient was dead of suffocation.

The memory makes McAslan's hackles rise, but he doesn't fume. His voice drops slightly in pitch and becomes icy calm. His hands rest lightly on the desktop. His eyes focus on a far corner, and his words are trimmed in Scottish. They are precise words, individual, each set apart from the next, all cast in iron and covered with chrome. He says he inquired as to the identify of the physician.

"I called him up and I complimented him on assisting in the procedure, but I had to point out that these troopers were trained to put a special device into the esophagus, and he had succeeded in taking it out and putting it in the trachea, where it wasn't meant to go, as a result of which the patient died. I suggested he make himself familiar with the device."

Upstairs, in the glassed-in SYSCOM booth, the dispatcher leans over the microphone, talking to helicopter four. There is a nice tailwind, and the helo pilot says he will deliver the Isolette and its occupant a little earlier than estimated. The dispatcher copies down the revised arrival time, signs off and reaches for the telephone dial.

Cowley was by no means the first doctor who wanted to use helicopters for ambulances. Other jurisdictions tried them, but they were too expensive. A helicopter crew could sit in a ready room for a week without a call, then get three on the same shift. Even as a lifesaving device, helicopters were not cost-effective.

But when the trauma docs and the state police went to the Department of Transportation together, they got helicopters. The state police were grateful, and the SYSCOM dispatcher never gets any argument.

On one occasion, a helicopter carrying the governor of Maryland landed immediately and told the chief executive to get out. The aircraft was needed for a medevac assignment. Standing by the roadside, the governor watched the helicopter disappear over the horizon.

That was one of Marvin Mandel's first contacts with Cowley's system and the people who were dying. He would have more. The growing storm at the University of Maryland and within the emergency medical community would soon spread all the way to the state capital and into the governor's ornate office.

"Boy," Mandel says, years later. "I think medical politics are much tougher than politics as I know it." Mandel, the acknowledged master of Maryland politics and the man who later would be sentenced to federal prison for racketeering and mail fraud, shakes his head and whistles. "Much tougher. They tried to make Dr. Cowley look like an individual who'd gone berserk, who was doing everything counter to what the medical profession would want to see. And, oh, God, they had meetings all over the place, denouncing him."

In SYSCOM, the radio tells the dispatcher that helo four is on the ground at City Hospital. The dispatcher makes notes.

In northeast Baltimore a baby is being born in an ambulance. The ambulance medic's voice is calm as he talks to the emergency room doctor on the radio, his voice backed up by the yelp of the siren.

"Helicopter one, SYSCOM."

The dispatcher reaches for the clipboard.

A moment later, the Shocktrauma unit's public address system clicks on. "THERE WILL BE AN ADMISSION IN FIVE MINUTES FROM THE BELTWAY, POSSIBLE C-SPINE."

The rubber soles of the admitting nurse's shoes squeak loudly as she runs across the tile.

21

THE SYSCOM DISPATCHER ROLLS HIS CHAIR FOR-
ward and with a sigh, picks up the VIP notification list.
A banker's wife. Protocol. The telephone rings in Cowley's tiny apartment and the dispatcher waits. Eight.
Nine. Ten. Cowley picks up the receiver. There is the
sound of a shower in the background. Cowley listens,
then grunts noncommittally into the telephone. Liz is
already on her way to work. Marianna Herschel, Cowley's public relations officer, is on her way to a legis-
lative hearing in Annapolis and stops to answer her
beeper from a telephone booth. She doesn't sound interested in Mary, but she thanks the dispatcher for notifying her.

Most medical institutions have VIP notification lists,
and sometimes a widely recognized name will get its
sick owner a politer doctor, a private room and a little
extra fussing.

In Shocktrauma, of course, such perks aren't really
relevant, and the patient usually isn't conscious enough
to care. Besides, unless a VIP is awake to brag about

it, as Mary was, the admitting team generally doesn't know who the patient is.

The VIP list does serve to alert Cowley and his staff to the possibility of widespread publicity. The Shock-trauma unit gets more than its share of newsworthy people, from high-ranking bureaucrats to notorious criminals. Upon the arrival of a patient like a Congressional staff-member who survived the Jonestown massacre in Guyanà, it may be necessary to take steps to keep reporters and camera crews out of the sterile areas.

It is equally important to the history of trauma medicine that the receipt of an influential victim often gives Cowley an opportunity to demonstrate the advantages of modern trauma care. A procession of well connected trauma victims have had a profound impact on the evolution of the Cowley brand of emergency medicine.

The VIP game is, however, common to the entire world of medicine. It often works to the advantage of the VIP, gaining him entrance to institutions like Johns Hopkins, the Mayo Clinic, Stanford, even the National Institutes of Health. Access to the doctors and scientists at those institutions contributes to the fact that VIPs tend to live longer than other people.

But fame tends to work against a trauma victim, and the celebrity who hits a tree somewhere in the Appalachians is almost certain to have his therapy bungled by amateurs.

Dr. Boyd, the government's top traumatologist, has some succinct advice for the famous. "Hospitals never give up a VIP," he says. "If you get injured, throw away your ID card and go the public route. You'll get better care."

The Shocktrauma unit has a long history of treating VIPs like everyone else, but its first one got an almost joyous welcome. Back in the early 1970s all of Cowley's patients were VIPs. He had so few.

The trauma unit was bright and new and almost empty. The doctors waited with nothing to do and the empty beds each chewed $500 a day out of Cowley's budget. The ambulance squads and local police refused to call the helicopters, and the emergency rooms seldom let go of a patient, famous or otherwise. Accident victims continued to die at the nearest hospital and community doctors prophesied that sooner or later the University of Maryland would get around to dealing with the would-be patient rustler and all his expensive, vacant beds. Cowley was worried.

Then, in the early morning hours of April 13, 1971, the inevitable happened.

Ex-Governor Marvin Mandel props his feet on his desk as he recalls the night. The legislature had adjourned well after midnight, following several intense days of scurrying to push through end-of-the-session bills. Everyone was exhausted. But tired or not James P. Mause, House Clerk and long-time friend of the then-governor, was anxious to get home to Frederick. Frederick was halfway across the state, but a police trooper was available to drive.

"I said, 'Don't drive home tonight,'" Mandel remembers. "'Stay over and go home first thing in the morning.' But he said no, he wanted to get home. I guess he left about two o'clock."

Mandel lights the meerschaum pipe that was his political trademark. "I guess about four o'clock in the morning I got a phone call that he had been in an automobile accident. The ambulance had taken him to a nearby hospital in Frederick."

The state police colonel told the governor he'd find out more about Mause's condition and call him back. When the officer dialed the governor's mansion about an hour later, Mandel answered on the first ring.

The governor learned that Frederick doctors had been unable to handle the patient and had sent him on to a somewhat larger hospital in Hagerstown. But a state police helicopter, with a trained medic aboard, was standing by to fly Mause to the trauma unit at the University of Maryland in Baltimore. A few minutes later, Mandel's state limousine sped north on Route 2, toward Baltimore.

Before the governor got anywhere near his destination, Mause's blanket-covered form rolled up the concrete ramp by the trash dumpster and followed the red line toward a waiting elevator.

The team leader looked at the injuries, took a deep breath, and went to work. Cowley got there a few minutes later.

"He'd been asleep in the front seat with his shoes off and his feet up on the dashboard," Cowley recalls. "He was sort of all scrunched up like that, asleep, when the state trooper who was driving him dozed off and hit a bridge abutment."

The trooper wasn't critically injured, but Mause was. The force of the impact broke his back, tore his knee joints from their sockets, ruptured several major blood vessels and crushed his chest. "He was in bad shape," one of the doctors remembers. "He was really a mess."

When the governor arrived, they wrapped a pink gown around his suit, put a paper cap on his head and gave him a face mask. He put it on and they led him into the blood-spattered first admitting area where his friend lay on the steel table, the respirator pumping air into his chest through a plastic fitting.

"He was lying flat," Mandel remembers. "I walked over to him and spoke to him. He was conscious, but he could hardly do anything but move his arms a little. I'll never forget that as long as I live. He indicated that he wanted a pad and pencil."

Slowly, with agonizing effort, Mause wrote: "Marvin, please, I want to live."

A long time has passed, and Mandel is quiet for a moment, looking at the wall. "You know," he says finally, "I still have that note someplace. You can imagine how it felt."

Afterward, Cowley ushered the governor outside. Mause would have to be taken over to University Hospital, to use one of their operating rooms. The operation, once it began, would probably be a long one. Perhaps Mandel should go home and get some sleep. No, Mandel said. There was no way he could sleep.

"So I stayed there," he remembers. "And I asked them to show me around a little bit."

Cowley led the governor, still shaken by the visit with his dying friend, all around the unit. The governor was awed.

"I saw a child that was about two years old, who had been in a bad fall. I saw another youngster there that had a bad burn. He showed me though the place and when I saw what was being done . . . it really struck me."

174

A few hours later, his adrenaline depleted, Mandel approached exhaustion and his staff took him home. As soon as he woke up, he returned. Cowley met him and informed him of Mause's condition, which was not good. Again, the politician and the doctor walked around the unit.

"Dr. Cowley...a totally dedicated individual. A man who, in his own field of heart surgery, was eminently successful. But he was totally dedicated to something different, to the Shocktrauma type of care. To him it was his whole life. And he was just trying to get that unit placed on sound footing without the hospital itself being his biggest enemy."

Jim Mause went from the operating room to the CCRU, and for days it looked like he would probably die. Mandel visited Mause every day. Cowley broke his own rule and let the governor in. Finally, one day, the surgeon told the governor that his friend would probably live, but in a wheelchair.

"They worked with him and worked with him," Mandel says, "and he survived. It was a long, drawn-out thing. I think his doctor bills were a hundred thousand dollars, but he lived. Today he's still in the wheelchair, but he's managed to overcome it all and he's still Clerk of the House.

"And during that period...it really struck me, the importance of having, immediately available, the trained people to get these victims to a hospital where they can get the kind of rapid treatment they urgently need. I don't know....

"Jim went to the Frederick hospital, and from the Frederick hospital to the Hagerstown hospital, and then

175

down to the Shocktrauma unit. Well, that couple of hours could have meant the difference between life and death, and it could have meant the difference between being paralyzed and not being paralyzed. If they had picked Jim up at the scene of the accident and got him to the Shocktrauma unit, it could be possible that he wouldn't be paralyzed. I don't know . . . but that's how I got interested in the whole situation."

The governor's interest would prove invaluable to Cowley later and, as his system grew, other VIPs added to its reputation. The son of the state's treasurer was flown to admitting with a tear in his aorta, the large artery of the heart. Quick diagnosis and surgery saved him. Reese D. Lofton, a Delta Airlines pilot whose body was riddled by a hijacker's dum-dum bullets, arrived in Admitting in full cardiac arrest, with damage to every one of his internal organs. He lived. Dutch Ruppersberger, with head and chest injuries that normally would have been fatal, still prosecutes white-collar criminals in Baltimore County. The front-page victories emphasized what good trauma medicine could do, but the medical community continued to embrace the nearest-hospital policy.

If the dying patients who came to Cowley survived to become living testimonials to his unit, the reverse was also true. Patients who were inadequately handled at the nearest hospital became object lessons.

When Arthur Bremer stepped smiling out of a crowd and pumped five shots into Alabama Governor George C. Wallace at a Laurel, Maryland shopping center in 1972, Dr. Boyd was still working on his trauma system in Illinois. He followed the story carefully from Chicago, and was horrified.

Cowley's helicopter system was cocked and ready, and the doctors were standing by in the admitting area. Governor Wallace, however, was loaded into the back of a station wagon, then manhandled into an ambulance with his wife, two Secret Service agents, a public relations man and eight other people. The medic didn't have enough maneuvering room to take a blood pressure reading.

The ambulance driver headed for Holy Cross Hospital, fifteen miles away in Silver Spring, where gunshot wounds were considered routine. In the preceding year, Holy Cross doctors had treated thirty-one of them.

Dr. Boyd, who in the same year supervised the care of more than eight thousand serious penetrating injuries, is blunt: "Besides the bad pre-hospital care, just the hospital care alone—they missed the obvious, did the wrong things and it came out like I predicted.

"He had stomach, pancreas, spinal cord and bowel injuries. I said, 'Oh shit. They will treat him there. They will call neurosurgical consultations from the University of Maryland, but they will not have a general surgical consultation. Everybody's a goddamned traumatologist, right?

"I predicted that he will either die or he will be in the intensive care unit for twenty-one days, and he will dehisce." He pronounces it *de-hiss*.

"You know what dehiscence is? The whole goddamned incision comes open and your guts are all over the floor. Well, he dehisced, and he got out of the intensive care unit—after serious septic episodes—on the twenty-second day. That's how close I called it."

Dr. Boyd, along with Cowley and other traumatologists, emphasizes that trauma care is a science, not an art.

Soon after the Wallace shooting, Dr. Boyd went to the governor of Illinois, Richard Ogilvie, and there was a big scene in his office. Dr. Boyd can be insistent.

"I said look, Dick, when you go out of state I'm going with you. Every goddamned one of these things, the Kennedys . . . from Garfield on through McKinley . . . has been a SNAFU." That summer was campaign time, and Ogilvie had his share of speaking obligations. Dr. Boyd went along on every trip as the governor's personal traumatologist.

"You'll never prevent it," Dr. Boyd reasons. "If they want you, they got you. So I wanted to be there."

Dr. Boyd was by no means the only one who analyzed Wallace's treatment and found it wanting. In Washington, a humbled Secret Service made new plans. Neatly-trimmed, conservatively-dressed men came to Baltimore to talk to Cowley behind closed doors.

Today, should the President of the United States be seriously injured at the White House, he would not be rushed to the nearest hospital. He would not be taken to Georgetown University, nor to the Naval Hospital in Bethesda, nor to the fledgling trauma unit at the Washington Hospital Center. As the presidential helicopter rose from the manicured White House lawn, the pilot would be talking to SYSCOM.

Eighteen minutes later the President would roll by the garbage dumpster and travel the red line to the elevators and up to the first floor. There he would be treated exactly the same as any of the twelve hundred other patients who come to the trauma unit every year.

Now, on the trauma center's fourth floor, the SYS-COM dispatcher acknowledges that the state police helicopter has touched down on the rooftop. He makes a note of the time. It is 7:27 A.M.

Standing in the cold downdraft, the admitting nurse can see through the aircraft's Plexiglass windows that the medic is forcing air into the patient's mouth with a black bag. If she asked, she would learn that the patient has no identification. But she doesn't have time to ask.

22

___

BOTTLES OF LIQUID HANG FROM GLEAMING RACKS
above the long steel table. Two nurses move around
Admitting one, checking supplies and equipment,
breaking out knives and needles as they follow their
memorized checklists. The team leader and two junior
surgeons lean against a metal workbench, paper masks
hanging loose around their necks. The admitting nurse
bursts through the stairwell doors, panting.

"High cord," she says. "They're bagging him."

Feminine fingers rip open green sterile packages. The
instruments glitter in the light. The team leader shouts
"Upstairs!" at the intercom. "Get me somebody from
neuro."

The elevator light turns green and the stretcher rolls
through the opening doors, surrounded by two ambulance attendants, the helicopter medic and the anesthesiologist. The anesthesiologist squeezes the black
bag that forces oxygen into the patient's lungs.

The tall man lies on his back on a plywood frame,
atop the stretcher cushions. Six sets of hands transfer

him, backboard and all, onto the table. The gray blanket slides away and the naked skin glows like alabaster under the intense illumination of the surgical light. Except for a smeared crimson handprint across his belly there is no blood.

He appears to be not yet thirty, and his pale winter skin stretches across hard muscle. Working carefully, the three nurses pull away the sliced-up remains of a gray pinstriped suit. It goes into a pile along with the pieces of blood-smeared motorcycle jacket and leather pants. The helicopter medic hands a briefcase to the admitting nurse. "He had it with him," the medic says. The nurse opens it. There is a stack of insurance agent's forms and a paper bag with two sandwiches inside. The nurse throws the briefcase on the pile.

"With this kind of high-C fracture," the team leader instructs the junior surgeons, "you won't need an anesthetic for the cutdowns."

The admitting team clusters around the patient, who has a plastic airway protruding from his mouth. Already, one surgeon slices into the base of the throat to install a more permanent respirator aperture. Another team member cuts into the right arm in search of an artery. Blood spatters onto the tile.

The team leader examines his patient carefully, probing at the belly and chest. There is little fat. When the anesthesiologist steps back to adjust the respirator, the surgeon bends over the face.

"You a football player?" the surgeon asks. "You look like you could be." The patient's blue pupils jump back and forth, but the body doesn't move.

"Wiggle your toes for me," the surgeon demands.

"Move your toes. Can you move your toes? Can you hear me? Blink your eyes if you can hear me."

The eyes stare.

"Blink," the surgeon commands.

Slowly, both eyes close and then open. Tears gather between the eyelids.

The surgeon puts his index finger in the palm of the alabaster man's hand. "Squeeze," he says, but there is no response.

He grasps a nipple between finger and thumb and pinches hard. The patient doesn't move. The surgeon walks away, leaving to the others the chore of attaching the monitors. Already the dot on the screen jumps with each heartbeat and a nurse records pressures from the Swan-Ganz catheter inside the heart. The team leader leans on the metal counter and puts his head in his hands.

The admission continues routinely. A woman in a pink smock and lead apron snaps X rays of the neck and a surgeon sloshes more antiseptic solution over the lower abdomen in preparation for the belly tap. As the scalpel touches flesh the skin parts and a layer of white fat flashes for a moment, then is obscured by welling blood. The supine body does not flinch. A nurse tapes a grease-penciled sign on the front of the hanging surgical light. The lettering says, *"I am awake and can hear anything you say."*

The neurosurgeon is tall and thin and carries his knee hammer in his back pocket. He jabs the patient with pins, orders him to wiggle his toes and clench his fists. The blue eyes follow the neurosurgeon, but the body remains still.

Standing in front of the X-ray film board, the neuro man and the team leader talk at length, the neurosurgeon's ball point pen tracing the fractures in the second and third cervical vertebrae. Those hollow bones, which protect the spinal cord as it enters the brain, are so obviously dislocated that the helicopter medic whistles.

"I guess I would have done him a favor by leaving him there," the policeman says.

Tex, sipping on a final cup of coffee and at last getting ready to leave, ambles out of the operating room area and pauses to look at the X rays. He observes that the fracture is the kind sought by professional hangmen.

The admitting nurse picks up a ringing yellow telephone. The SYSCOM dispatcher says there is another case on the way, this one a transfer patient. A few minutes later, Tex, who has stayed around a minute too long, is drafted into the backup admitting team when the transfer patient arrives in the overflow area, wrapped in a wool blanket.

Tex examines the new arrival carefully while the rest of the team works frantically to force blood into her veins. Her pressure is low and her heartbeats are rapid, too rapid. Tex examines the fresh, neatly-stitched surgical gash that runs up her abdomen. She's obviously a teenager, and just as obviously in deep shock. The surgeon reads the hospital transfer records, puzzled.

"It looks like she was bleeding in her belly and they didn't figure it out," he says aloud to the team. He flips to another page of the record and his baffled expression changes to a frown. "I wonder why the hell they waited so long?"

Tex walks to the head of the table and leans over the patient's ear. "Linda?" he says.

Nothing.

Outside the overflow area, people in pink gowns gravitate toward the X-ray board. One nurse stands on her toes to get a look at the film. Everybody wants to see the hangman's fracture.

Downstairs, the team leader learns, the man's parents are in the waiting room, and his pregnant wife is on the way. The surgeon walks away from the X-ray board, leans against a tile wall and rests his eyes on the artificially inflating chest of the alabaster man.

Evolution arranged that all human nerve pathways converge at the base of the neck and travel, together, through the top few joints of vertebrae. Information from the fingertips, motion from the pumping chest, pleasure from the genitals, hunger from the stomach and fullness from the colon are all sensations that are relayed through the delicate rope of nerves that, according to the X-ray films, has been severed. At the very top of the broken rope, entombed in the alabaster body, a frantic, blue-eyed mind is even now spinning off into madness.

23

THE HOSPITAL SITS BACK FROM THE ROAD, BEYOND
a yew hedge and across a rolling expanse of frozen lawn.
The aluminum and glass facade shines in the bright
winter sun. A florist's truck stands, unattended, near
the entrance.

Inside the automatic doors a nurse in a starched white
uniform waits behind a patient in a wheelchair. The
thick carpet absorbs the soothing music from the loudspeakers and two gray-haired women in crisp volunteer
uniforms help the florist arrange three bowls of cut
flowers on a walnut coffee table. Behind the lobby,
beyond a set of stainless steel doors, two men lean
against a countertop and converse in quiet tones.

"He was right, you know," the younger man says,
rubbing a paper-booted foot against the opposite leg of
his surgical scrub pants and looking down into his empty
coffee cup. "I should have done a belly tap."

The other man, taller and balding, shakes his head
emphatically. "No," he says. "I mean, maybe. In hindsight, that's easy to say. Nevertheless, he was clearly

out of line to make the kind of statements . . . the kind of accusations . . . he did. If you don't report it, then I will. Personally, I make it a point not to accept calls from there if I can avoid it."

"He was right, though," the younger man persists stubbornly, breaking off a small piece of Styrofoam from the lip of his empty cup and dropping it down inside. "I did a thorough examination. The belly was completely unremarkable and she was sitting up and talking on the telephone. But I should have done a belly tap."

Another Styrofoam chip goes into the cup.

"Look," the older man says, forcefully. "It is not an acceptable practice to do surgical procedures on everyone who walks in the door. The department has been over that. It's a question of policy. What happened was unfortunate, but I'd strongly advise you against making up policy as you go along."

Another Styrofoam chip, then another and another.

Finally, the younger man shrugs and looks at his watch. Slowly, he stoops to strip the soiled paper booties from his shoes. He deposits them in a trash can, along with the disassembled coffee cup, as he leaves.

24

THE FIRST WISPS OF SELF-AWARENESS FLOAT IN
a bubble of pain, a symphony of pain that crawls up
the arms and legs and crashes through the chest and
belly in great shuddering waves that never stop.
Thought flickers briefly between the waves, and is en-
gulfed.

There are no distractions from the pain. Larry floats
atop a "puff pack" mattress composed of hundreds of
soft foam rubber fingers. His heels, where they touch
the bed, are protected with fleece pads. His wrists are
tied to the bed railings with soft wrappings of gauze.
Even his breath is disembodied and beyond his control,
governed by the Engstrom respirator, bypassing his
mouth, nostrils and voice box, entering his chest at the
base of his throat through an opening that hurts.

Pain. And no way to scream.

The human brain evolved to fit the needs of a simpler
animal . . . a durable animal, up to a point. It could
survive a broken leg or a gouged-out eye. Pain served
to keep the animal still, so healing could proceed, and

if the shock became too deep, the brain winked off first. It was never designed to wink back on.

Dr. Schnaper could not resist.

Nathan Schnaper is a psychiatrist who is drawn to death. Like Elizabeth Kubler-Ross, he specializes in the dying mind, but unlike Elizabeth Kubler-Ross, he has nothing nice to say about death. He sees no evidence that dying is pleasant. Quite the contrary.

In the years he spent at the trauma unit, Dr. Schnaper compiled detailed notes and collected case histories to piece together an in-depth analysis of how it feels to be pulled back from death by a trauma nurse. He says the abyss between patient and nurse is awesome.

The nurse can move around, scratch her nose, talk and, in a few hours, go home. The patient can do none of these things. Helplessness, and the pain, reduce the trauma patient to infancy.

It's not uncommon, Dr. Schnaper says, to see a semiconscious patient's hand work its way out of its bindings and move toward his genitals. "A small child does the same thing," the psychiatrist explains. "Masturbation is a release of tension. It feels good, reassuring. It is an infantile, self-comforting act."

One of Dr. Schnaper's favorite observation posts is the island in the CCRU. From there, he can watch the doctors and the nurses, as well as the patients.

"The trauma patient is in a cocoon," Dr. Schnaper says, thoughtfully, his eyes resting on a teenager's body. "They withdraw because they're bombarded. They see people who are masked and gowned and capped. There are the monitors. There are the alarm bells going off, and the respirators and the lights . . . it's like a war bunker."

The nurse moves around the boy purposefully, adjusting the flow of intravenous liquid and checking the monitors. Though he does not appear conscious, she talks softly to him, and often touches him, maternally.

"When you talk to these patients later they don't remember much," Dr. Schnaper says. "What they remember is like a dream, a fantasy. Their unconscious minds fill that void in consciousness with fantasy, and three things evolve.

"One is that they're being held prisoner. That makes sense, because they're tied down with tubes and catheters in them and so on. But each patient justifies his imprisonment with his own fantasies, and that's the second thing.

"One woman, an elderly widow, thought she was being held to be sold into white slavery. She wanted to tell them it was ridiculous, she was too old. But, of course, she couldn't tell them anything because she couldn't talk. She was on the respirator.

"Another guy thought he had taken his dump truck and run over a bus load of school children and killed a car full of pregnant women. Each one finds a way to justify the imprisonment.

"The third thing is that no patient has ever told me he experienced a state of death. Often, they were not sure whether they were alive or dead, though. Some used different ways to try to find out. Some would count and say to themselves, I'm thinking, therefore I am. One woman tried to urinate, on the theory that if you have a bodily function you're alive. The ironic thing, of course, is that she had a catheter in place so she couldn't tell."

The essential weirdness of the trauma patient's surroundings gives shape to the hallucinations, but the basic disorientation grows from more fundamental, physical problems.

Of all the organs in the body, the brain is the one most susceptible to shock and, even within the brain itself, there is a hierarchy of endurance. The higher centers, where conscious thought is processed, shut off as soon as blood pressure drops, while the brain stem, which sits atop the spinal cord and controls basic functions like breathing, may continue to operate even after the rest of the brain is irrevocably dead.

Nowhere in the body is the cellular disorganization that follows shock so apparent as in the recovering mind. All cells talk to each other with chemical impulses but, within the brain, those conversations compose an exceedingly complex chemical ballet.

In the post-shock brain, the cells themselves are slow and awkward, and patterns are disorganized. Information itself becomes garbled. The pilot who was shot by a hijacker lay in an isolation room and decided that he was in the airport cafeteria. Sometimes his scenery would inexplicably shift and he would lie in bed adjusting imaginary cockpit dials, switches, instruments and levers.

The trauma patient's disorientation serves to remind the surgeon that communication breakdowns are occurring all over the body. Since few of those more subtle networks can be monitored, the doctor shies away, when possible, from administering painkillers.

Besides, it is always safer to deal with a patient who is awake and alert, pain or no pain. If something goes wrong, diminished consciousness can serve as an early warning signal.

Finally, and more practically, Tex wonders if the pain won't help Larry wake up. He has been unconscious for five days now. Medically, it would be better to prescribe no morphine at all. . . .

But there's the pain.

Tex balances the conflicting demands as Freckles stands before him, insistent. Tex suggests he should wait a while. Freckles says no, now. Right now.

Tex looks at her. She's convinced, and that tells Tex what he needs to know. Okay, he says, okay, and he writes a standing order for morphine.

For three days, Larry had lain still in the bed and then, yesterday, his arms began to pull mindlessly against the restraints. Today the movements became more purposeful and began to be accompanied by a racing of the heart. Pain.

Freckles inserts the needle into a plastic intravenous tube and injects the morphine into the flow. The painkiller mingles with the saline solution as it flows into the bloodstream, travels to the heart, through the lungs and up the carotid arteries into the brain. The pain subsides and the heartbeat slows.

Freckles moves gracefully around the fragile nude body. There is a procedure for everything, passed from senior to junior trauma nurse in the form of choreography. Their bodies flow like dancers, fluid and constant. Throughout the unit pink-gowned, paper-capped nurses are in motion. Their hands hang bottles, turn valves, measure secretions and scribble notes.

In cubicle twelve, a young woman who grew up in the wealthy northern suburbs of Baltimore plunges a needle into the heroin-scarred vein of a black man her own age. In cubicle seven, a pair of hazel eyes surrounded by purple makeup focus intently on a vial of dark urine. There is little evidence here of the everyday tumble of random events that prevails outside, in the real world. Out there, precision is an advertisement and a dream. In Shocktrauma, it is an ambition.

Hours later, Larry's eyes open slowly. They do not focus.

Freckles studies the open eyes. Did the eyes move in their sockets, or was that an illusion?

"Hi, Larry," she says, loudly, bending over his ear. There is no response.

"Hi, Larry," the nurse repeats. "I sure am glad you woke up. Do you know where you are? You're in the hospital. I know you can't talk, but stick out your tongue if you hear me."

Freckles watches. There is no movement. Still . . .

Turning to the counter, the nurse prints a sign on a piece of typing paper with a Magic Marker. The sign says, "My name is Larry. I am awake and can hear anything you say." She tapes it up in the back of the cubicle, where it can be seen by everyone in the area, except Larry.

Nearby there is another sign, an official one, that says the boy's physician is Tex and that his primary nurse is Freckles. There were words about that with the nurse chairman.

It had seemed a natural thing to do. Since by a fluke Freckles had admitted this patient and later had a chance to treat him upstairs . . . it seemed rational to put herself down as his primary nurse. After all, she knew his history. But when the shift changed last Saturday morning, she'd worked sixteen hours straight. She collapsed in a chair in the nurses' lounge, and the fatigue must have shown.

Even so, it would have escaped notice, except for the uncomfortable fact that Freckles and her supervisor had had a long talk two weeks before on the subject of Freckles's work habits. The nurse-chairman had noticed Freckles's increasing tendency to take on too much responsibility, too many jobs. The nurse-chairman was right, and Freckles knew it. That's why she'd gone for the idea of moving downstairs to Admitting.

But, she tried to explain to the nurse-chairman in the lounge that Saturday, there were circumstances . . . she was coming back upstairs anyway for two weeks, and why not . . .

When she said it out loud, the excuse sounded very flimsy. Pressing hard, the nurse-chairman had even forced her to admit that. Nevertheless, she didn't erase her primary nurse assignment off the blackboard, and neither did the nurse-chairman.

After all, Freckles was as qualified as anyone.

It is 3:30 P.M., almost time for Freckles to go home, when the eyes open again. This time the eyeballs move, unmistakably.

"Larry?" Freckles says.

The eyes shift, very slowly, toward the source of the sound.

"Larry, you had an accident. You're in the hospital. Do you understand that, Larry? If you can understand me, stick out your tongue."

Slowly, slowly, the lips open and the teeth part and the tongue moves, but there is no strength to extend it.

"That's good, Larry. That's very good. I talked to your mom and dad earlier today. They can't visit you right now, but they said to tell you that they love you."

The boy's mouth opens and his throat strains to speak, but there is no air. The respirator bypasses the vocal cords. The attempt brings pain and the boy grimaces.

Carefully, Freckles unties the boy's right hand and puts a pencil in it. The pencil is held against a pad of paper, and the nurse amplifies the hand's feeble attempt to write. The lines jerk and wave on the paper, but the word is readable. The word is, "Linda."

Larry's eyes are filled with pain, but they focus. Freckles doesn't turn away, but she hesitates.

"I'll call your parents and try to find out," she finally says. It is impossible to tell whether the boy's disordered mind detected the hesitation. He has no way to scream.

25

_____

THROUGHOUT THE HISTORY OF MEDICINE, THE nurse's role has been principally that of a servant. Almost always, the nurse was a she, and she changed sheets, emptied bedpans, brought meals, cleaned, turned, stepped and fetched. When technology became more sophisticated, the nurse studied and coped, but her role didn't change . . . nor did her pay.

In the 1960s, as medical technology exploded and hospitals grew, the relationship between effort and remuneration in the nursing profession reached a breakpoint. Thousands of nurses, whose wages were generally below the official federal poverty level, left nursing for better paying jobs. Nurses disappeared from the hospitals at about the same time, and for many of the same reasons, that servants disappeared from the suburbs.

Suddenly, the crisis was acute. Patients died because there weren't enough nurses. At University Hospital, it was not uncommon for one registered nurse to be in charge of two entire floors, with the direct patient care being provided by licensed practical nurses who were paid minimum wage. Doctors who could find and keep nurses could treat their patients effectively. Those who couldn't, couldn't.

Cowley was bullheaded about the problem. In the long nights sitting up with his shock patients, he had learned to appreciate the minute-to-minute nursing technology that sometimes helped the dying patient live on, and on, and on, and on, and sometimes even recover. That's the technology he'd banked on for the death lab, and he intended to have it.

He couldn't pay extra money to his nurses, because the university wouldn't allow it, so he offered them the only thing of value he had to give: his knowledge. Many times he'd absently begun explaining the details of physiology to nurses and, each time he caught himself doing so, he noted that the nurse was listening. He watched, fascinated, as the nurses he talked to applied their knowledge. He began taking nurses with him on his morning rounds, explaining, teaching . . . cultivating.

If his nurses worked harder, he compensated them with harder work. He taught them procedures that nurses elsewhere were forbidden to perform. They learned the fundamentals of diagnosis, how to make the most of electronic medicine, when and how to place an intravenous line and the techniques of resuscitating a dying patient. After a grueling day of work, Cowley and his nurses would spend additional hours in the classroom. The nurses went home with books.

Cowley fought for his nurses, coddled them, protected them and, when he could afford it, took them to dinner. Coincidentally, the recovery rate among his patients soared. As he matured as a surgeon and scientist, he gathered around him a small cadre of uniquely trained, highly temperamental and fiercely loyal nurses.

Liz was one of the first, and she stayed the longest. She became Cowley's senior nurse and they would work late into the night, researching shock, talking about the process of death. Clearly, it could be reversed only with constant, skilled bedside care by a trained nurse. Ultimately it was the nurse, not the doctor, who was always there.

"Today, in trauma medicine, the nurse has become a doctor," Cowley says. "She's deciding. She's making decisions. This always pisses Liz off . . . but I call them my little doctors." In the more than twenty years since Cowley began to assemble his first nursing team, he has become increasingly adamant about the importance of bedside care. And he makes certain the young surgeons who work in the trauma unit are aware of his views.

The way he computes it, Shocktrauma attracts some of the world's top young surgeons. From among the applicants, Cowley chooses the best. He can get all the surgeons he wants. Each incoming class of Fellows gets a fair warning.

It is a standard speech, and Cowley delivers it every July in the upstairs classroom where doctors meet for rounds.

"We do a lot of thing differently here," Cowley tells them, "and one of the things that's different is the nursing program. I want you to understand right now that these nurses are not your employees. They are your colleagues, and right now they know more about trauma medicine than you do. I expect them to be treated accordingly."

Out on the floor, the nurses assume the young doctors are attentive. Those who aren't get an ego-bruising reminder.

Under the law of Maryland, and of other states, it is not legal for a nurse to prescribe an antibiotic for her patient when his temperature rises. Instead, she has to ask a doctor to prescribe. Sometimes trauma nurses are in a rush, and sometimes they don't ask as sweetly as the nurses did at the young doctor's last hospital. And then sometimes, as a defensive gesture, the doctor balks.

While it is illegal for the nurse to prescribe the antibiotic, it is not at all against the law for her to understand, in intricate detail, the biochemical processes that express themselves in the fever that follows shock. It is not her responsibility if the physician knows less about the subject than she does. Being instructed by one's juniors can be an edifying and often even enlightening experience for a doctor, and some nurses are meaner than others.

"Sometimes it gets to be very difficult," says Liz. "If you get a doctor who is very defensive and a nurse who is very castrating, you run into a lot of problems. In some cases, especially with the new Fellows and residents, the nurses know a heck of a lot more than they do, and it's not supposed to be within their job description to know more than the doctor.

"A physician can begin to wonder," she adds. "What the hell am I supposed to do? She knows as much as I do. Why did I have to go through so many years of school . . . ?"

The unusual power wielded by Shocktrauma nurses has emboldened them to attack a variety of rather obvious human problems that the doctors had somehow overlooked. The primary nursing program, for instance, began when a trauma nurse became friends with a woman who had lost her arm in an automobile accident. Some weeks after the patient was released from the hospital, the nurse visited her at home and was stunned to find her trying to peel a potato with one hand. She'd received the best trauma care in the world, yet nobody had thought to tell her about prosthetic arms!

Soon, the nurses began assigning one of their number to be personally responsible for each patient who entered the unit. That nurse became a one-woman oversight committee and patient advocate.

As the patient lies in his cubicle, his life is maintained by a series of nurses who come and go with each shift change, but one face, that of the primary nurse, appears again and again.

As Larry's primary nurse, for instance, Freckles makes sure his individual needs don't get lost in the impersonal medical machinery of the Shocktrauma unit. She checks his medication schedule and recommends two changes to Tex, who gracefully agrees. Freckles knows about Larry's three cocker spaniels and his interest in history, and she'll use that knowledge later to help bolster his courage.

Today, Freckles's primary nurse responsibilities keep her three-quarters of an hour beyond her shift, talking to Larry's parents in the hallway downstairs. They have just met with Linda's primary nurse, and their eyes are red.

"Please," Freckles pleads for her patient, "think about your son, too. Be happy he's waking up and understand . . . he's asking questions about his sister. You've got to let me tell him."

"No," the man says again. The mother stands beside him in silent agreement.

"At least let me tell him she's here, then," Freckles says.

"No."

"But he's starting to ask. He's asked four times. I had to tell him something and . . . I said she's in the hospital, and that he shouldn't worry. That's sort of not true, I can't lie to him. I shouldn't. He's got to have a chance to deal with it. Think about how he must feel."

"No," the father says.

Freckles knows the family's terms. Let them visit Larry, and they'll tell him themselves.

"No," Freckles says, again. "I . . . just . . . can't."

After Larry's parent leave, Freckles sits in the nurses' lounge and smokes three cigarettes, one after another. She should have just told him. She shouldn't have said anything about it to the parents. She should have known better. It might be nice to be in charge of a small, quiet, modern emergency room somewhere. Again, she reaches into her uniform pocket and touches the folded-up letter. After a while, she changes into street clothes and goes home and her cigarette, forgotten on a dirty glass plate, continues to burn until it reduces itself to a long gray ash.

If the nurses control the unit, it also controls them

and they pay the price in stress. Liz Scanlan was struggling with burnout long before the phenomenon became the subject of cocktail party conversations.

"We have a difficult patient population to work with, because the patients are in the nurse's own age group," Liz says. "They may be dying, and they got hurt doing the same things these nurses do every day. It's different for a doctor, a doctor comes and goes, but the nurse has to work with the patient for eight hours at a time, and she gets totally involved."

The high stress and heavy responsibilities lead to a rapid turnover of the nursing staff. The new nurses arrive fresh and enthusiastic, and then, sometimes, leave . . . shellshocked . . . after just a few months. Few stay more than three years.

In an attempt to identify and correct incipient burnout, designated senior nurses keep an eye on their colleagues. They watch especially for the harshness and apathy that characterize emotional overload, and for the excessive responsibility-taking that leads ultimately to exhaustion and flight.

Freckles liked the idea of going downstairs. In Admitting the tension swings from zero to intolerable in a few seconds, but it always swings back. Upstairs, it is a constant grind that soon becomes habit, and then the backdrop of existence. Freckles had watched herself becoming withdrawn, avoiding the company of other CCRU nurses, and she recognized that as a danger sign.

Still, she didn't know the senior woman was so concerned. Saturday, the nurse-chairman had used the word "compulsive" three times, and she'd looked frankly exasperated.

Over the years, Liz Scanlan discovered that dealing with trauma nurses was a tricky, tricky business. "You have to treat 'em as pedigreed dogs," she says, slightly embarrassed. "They were good nurses to start with and then we trained them, and we've got to keep them. So we do whatever we have to."

For Cowley's part, protecting nurses is a way of life that sometimes blurs into his own Mormonesque version of chivalry. Cowley is the kind of old-fashioned gentlemen who hesitates and agonizes before telling an off-color joke to a mixed audience. Once, when a less circumspect young doctor tangled with one of Liz's nurses, Cowley called the entire medical staff into the small second-floor conference room.

He was obviously angry. He paced, searching for words. He spoke evenly about the pressures of the trauma business, and of the tendency for tempers to flare. He understood this, he said, but ... the words became more elusive and his face grew redder and redder. Finally, his heavy fist slammed down on the table and he bellowed in a voice that carried the length of the long hallway. "BUT IF I EVER HEAR OF ANYONE EVER CALLING ONE OF MY NURSES A FUCKING CUNT AGAIN THAT PERSON WILL BE GONE THE NEXT DAY!"

For a long moment, he stood there, glaring at the cringing doctors. Then he stomped out.

Most of the time, however, the nurses solve their own problems in simple and direct fashion. The legends include the time a young surgeon, bending over a dying patient in the operating room, refused again and again to give up. Finally the unit's clinical director, who is

202

theoretically Cowley's second-in-command, fired him over the intercom.

The nurses in the operating room thought the punishment was too harsh. The next day an ad-hoc committee of nurses sent an ultimatum to Cowley, and the day after that the surgeon was back at work.

The nurses are not flattered by Cowley's description of them as "little doctors." They see themselves as something quite different, and Liz is sometimes miffed by Cowley's inability to understand that nurses are interested in what they call "hands-on" care. They want to do nursing, not doctoring, and their chief demand is that the doctors steer clear of things they don't understand.

One clinical director, who apparently took his job title literally, posted a memo proclaiming a minor change in the nursing procedures. The nurses stood around the bulletin board, speculating on why the clinical director's name, and not Liz's, was at the bottom of the proclamation. The next day, a memo from Liz, instructing them to ignore the clinical director's orders, cleared the matter up.

In a few weeks, that particular clinical director cleaned out his office and left for a more traditional job elsewhere.

26

LONG BEFORE TOMMY COULD DRIVE, HE LOVED fast cars. When he was old enough, he worked part-time in gasoline stations to buy his first one and his parents chipped in, on the condition that the automobile have a roll bar and a good seat belt. If Tommy had been wearing that belt one night the week before, he would have been working at the station today. Instead, he lies alone in cubicle ten, with a tiny monitor wire running from beneath the spinal-fluid-soaked turban that covers the top of his head.

His heartbeat, according to the television monitor, is strong but slow, and his blood pressure is normal. The only strikingly unusual set of numbers is the one that appears on the instrument that connects to the sensor under the turban. The pressure within Tommy's head is far too high, but the fact attracts no attention. The respirator works rhythmically and his chest rises and falls.

The physique that stretches beneath the dripping bags and flashing monitors is long and muscular. The calloused hands are those of a mechanic and the forearms are sinewy, with protruding veins. There is a short stubble of beard on his chin and, beneath the closed eyelids, the pupils are dilated and unreactive to light. A large catheter protrudes from the tip of his penis and carries normal quantities of yellow fluid into the urine bag.

The body is not gruesomely marked. It took only a single blow to kill Tommy, the contact of skull against rock in a boulder field beyond a long curve in a country road.

Back up that road, on a hilltop, there was an old barn where the young men with hot cars brought their friends to drink beer and amuse themselves with loud music and louder engines.

Between the barn and the curve was a series of three sharp dips that could make a fast car leap into the air. The rollercoaster, as it was called, was a consummate test of driving skill, and on some nights carloads of teenagers roared down the narrow highway, laughing and shrieking.

The rollercoaster's last thrill came at the end, where the unbanked road swept to the right and the cars fishtailed, tires squealing on the macadam. Occasionally a car lost control at this point and slid into the rocky field beyond. A sixteen-year-old boy died there last summer, and the death increased the renown of the rollercoaster.

Tommy's car remained relatively intact as it rammed through the barbed wire fence and into the field, but the door popped open and Tommy flew out, cracking his head against a rounded granite outcropping. The impact drove the upper plates of his skull down against his brain.

Thirteen automobiles and more than fifty teenagers stood by as the helicopter landed at the curve of the road. They were surprised. Tommy was a good driver. The admitting team leader, when he discovered the patient's blood-alcohol content, wasn't surprised at all.

Remarkably, Tommy continued to breathe. Though the brain cells that contained his personality died in the boulder field, the deeper circuits that program life functions were rescued by the helicopter medic. The admitting team labored all night and a CCRU nurse worked throughout the next day before the obvious became the inescapable. At that juncture, the nurses found it efficient to place Tommy next to Christine.

Her monitors, like Tommy's, all show normal readings except for the one that expresses intracranial pressure. The blonde hair is gone now, and the sensor, which resembles a small spark plug, protrudes from the top of her bald skull. In a classic response, her hands have twisted outward and become clawlike. Her feet twist down and outward.

The monitors tell the story, neatly. The skull is not, in literal fact, a closed box. There is a one-inch opening at the bottom, where the spinal cord enters, and rising intracranial pressures have squeezed the bottom of her brain through that hole like so much watery gray toothpaste.

A full bag of urine hangs beneath Christine's bed. Every two hours an attendant methodically turns both Tommy and Christine.

The state of Maryland was one of the first in the nation to recognize what had been a scientific fact for decades: The brain is the mechanism of individuality and when it dies, the citizen is dead.

On two successive days, electroencephalograms failed to reveal any electrical activity inside either of the two patients' skulls. A parade of young neurosurgeons visited the adjacent cubicles to stand at the foot of the beds and scrape their metal hammer handles over the soles of the feet. The men dug their fingers deeply into the insides of the thighs, searing for a nerve that might produce enough pain to evoke a twitch. They twisted nipples and pressed on eyeballs. Nothing. Finally a senior physician made notes in each patient record and the deaths became official. The nurses would have switched off the respirators then, were it not for the yellow urine that continued to flow into the collection bags. Two brains were dead but four kidneys were not.

Now the trauma nurses continue to watch the monitors and adjust the flow of intravenous liquids. They keep the hearts beating and the blood chemistries within normal range and they change the dressings regularly. A warm corpse is an invitation to bacteria.

27

BEFORE THE HELICOPTERS STARTED FLYING IN 1968, some accident victims were simply ... expendable. The equipment and skills necessary to save them were available in large medical centers, but they weren't cost-effective in the suburban emergency room. Often, when the injuries were subtle, the diagnosis was made at autopsy.

The young police officer in Admitting one is in obvious pain from his broken ribs but the team leader can find no serious injuries. His blood gases are a little low, but that's not abnormal for a smoker. There is no obvious reason to believe there is any blood in the belly.

In fact, the surgeon is beginning to suspect that the patient's repeated pleas to be sent home are not totally unreasonable, and if he were still working in the New England hospital where he had done his residency, he'd put the patient to bed and have a nurse check on him through the night. On the face of the evidence, the man shouldn't be here at all.

Since he's here, however, the team leader is obliged to assume the worst and follow Cowley's protocol.

The accident happened as the policeman chased a speeder through the countryside just outside the city. Suddenly the speeder lost his nerve and hit his brakes. The cruiser swerved, missing the stopped car and smacking into a telephone pole. The officer unbuckled his seat belt and crawled through the window, cursing, and anywhere else he'd have been taken to the nearest emergency room.

But in Maryland, police departments were among the first governmental organizations to appreciate the implications of Cowley's system. Time and time again, the state troopers loaded obviously dying drivers into the helicopter and then, two months later, those same troopers met the victims, alive and well, in court. Word got around, and now the police reaction is to summon a helicopter anytime one of their own is injured. They see no reason why they should fail to benefit from a medical system that repeatedly saved the lives of drunks, riffraff and common criminals.

That is all very abstract to the surgeon and the cop who demands, again, to go home. He wants codeine for the ribs, something to wear—the admitting nurse cut off a perfectly good uniform—and a taxi. His principal worry is that the police chief is going to make him pay for the cruiser and the splintered telephone post.

The admitting nurse soothes him frequently and ineffectively. "Just be quiet now and be a good boy for us," she says. "I know it hurts, but we have to do a few more things to make sure you're okay. We're going to sit you up and take an X ray now."

Again the cop asks for something for the pain in his ribs and again the anesthesiologist explains to him that he'll have to wait. If the patient suddenly starts getting groggy, the anesthesiologist doesn't want to wonder whether the change is caused by painkillers or by shock.

The patient gasps with pain as the nurses sit him up and put a large gray plate behind him. The X-ray technician adjusts her machine's cross-hairs on the center of the chest, the way the late radiologist Dr. Robert Ayella taught her.

He was a good teacher, but it wasn't his teaching that earned him a place in medical history. It was his ingeniously simple idea that a chest X ray of a sitting patient could help diagnose a condition with only one previously-known symptom—sudden death.

It was an approach well suited to Cowley's shock-trauma unit, where doctors weren't allowed to second-guess the state trooper. The doctor wasn't at the scene; the state trooper was. He looked at the demolished car and decided that if the patient wasn't a multiple trauma victim, he was luckier than a statistical universe usually allows.

Back in New England, the team leader would call for consultations, but here he doesn't have that option. Here he has a protocol. So he waits, impatiently, for the upright chest X ray to be processed.

Cowley's discovery in the death lab was that shock is a predictable disease as well as a rapid one. That meant the thinking had to be done in advance, and that meant protocols. Trauma, the heart surgeon tried to tell his critics, wasn't like other diseases.

It was a difficult message to get across. Cowley's peers were accustomed to patients with more insidious pathologies, like atherosclerosis and cancer. A cancer patient benefitted from bedside debate between internists, pharmacologists and oncologists. So did the doctors, each of whom rendered separate bills, and they saw no reason to credit Cowley's argument to anything other than greed.

Cowley responded to the pressure by digging in. On several occasions, Shocktrauma doctors bodily ejected outside physicians who tried to meddle. In the trauma unit, if nowhere else, the protocols stood.

Now, in the admitting area, the team doctors stand in front of the X ray of the policeman's chest, talking with excitement. The team leader invokes Dr. Ayella's name, twice.

In hindsight, it makes sense. They only talk for a minute, and then they move.

The patient is transferred to a bed with wheels. A nurse, the team leader, a second surgeon and the anesthesiologist push the bed and an attendant trots behind. The elevators are excruciating slow. The surgeon mentally reviews the procedures for opening a chest under unsterile conditions.

The policeman is confused and growing frightened, and the nurse attempts to comfort him. The hospital's sophisticated X-ray unit is only a hallway away.

The aorta is the largest artery in the human body. It rises out of the heart in a long graceful curve back toward the spine, where it disappears into the inner wall of the chest cavity. It is a strong vessel composed, like a good garden hose, of several layers. The inside lining is a coating of smooth tissue, wrapped with a second layer of muscle. Over the outside of the artery stretches a thin but very tough sheath.

Occasionally, when the force of a collision throws a driver's body forward against the seat belt or the steering wheel, the heart continues forward and slams into the front of the chest. The muscular heart can absorb the blow, but its sudden movement can tear the aorta where it's fastened to the chest wall.

Generally, only two of the three arterial layers will tear. The elastic covering can stretch and can even sustain, for a while, the pressures generated by the pounding heart. But inevitably the sheath grows tired, loses its tone, and balloons outward. In an hour, or three, it ruptures. The patient loses consciousness instantly and dies in four minutes, his chest full of spurting blood. There was only one apparent symptom of a ruptured aorta, and that symptom was death.

Now, in the specialized X-ray room, the trauma team seeks to verify the diagnosis. The instruments whine loudly as the radiologist pushes a plunger and the dye shoots into the injured policeman's artery. The dye streams out into the aorta. The machine clicks. The team leader examines the X ray and his own heart pounds. The patient's aorta is the size of a fist.

Moments later, a trauma unit chest surgeon answers his beeper. Interrupting a conversation with two senior doctors, he runs down the stairs, two and sometimes three at a time. In a hallway near the medical school X-ray department, the rolling bed delivers a glancing blow to an ashtray stand and sand spills on the polished tile. The attendant holds the elevator door open.

The team leader closes his eyes in the elevator and flexes his fingers. He would make the incision on the left side, a long, deep gash, big enough to reach into the chest, push by the lungs and pinch off the aorta above the tear. That would deny blood to the kidneys, liver and spinal cord, but it might save the brain. He would have to stop the bed, but it would be quick, and then they could roll again. The surgeon would run beside the bed, his hand inside the chest.

The policeman now fights the team, terrified. "Lay down," the team leader yells at him as the elevator doors open. The anesthesiologist presses a hypodermic plunger and the policeman turns confused, then unconscious.

In the operating room hallway the chest surgeon scrubs. Outside, the chest X ray still hangs on the admitting area light board and the trauma unit's X-ray technician is explaining its significance to a radiology student.

In the days when Maryland's accident victims were still being taken to the nearest emergency room, the only way a ruptured aorta could be detected was with a dye injected and an aortagram. That presupposes the availability of sophisticated equipment and poses a small but very real risk to the patient. Even if he had the equipment, which he usually didn't, the emergency room doctor couldn't ethically check every trauma patient . . . ruptured aortas are too uncommon. It was a problem that nagged at Dr. Ayella's mind.

Dr. Ayella, a diminutive man, who remained addicted to radiological puzzles and eighteen-hour days despite two heart attacks, was one of the few University of Maryland physicians who could share Cowley's vision.

The challenge was a diagnostic one. Any competent heart surgeon could replace the aorta with a length of Dacron tubing. But how could discovery be made in time without exposing the patients to undue risk? For years Dr. Ayella mused over the admission chest X rays of patients who had later died of undiagnosed ruptured aortas.

Such X rays, taken with the often-unconscious patient lying in a supine position, showed the clear images of both lungs as well as the pear-shaped shadow of the heart that lay pumping between them. The bulging bag behind was obscured by that shadow. Dr. Ayella found no diagnostic clues in the X rays.

The clue came instead from his own inductive questions and his knowledge of anatomy.

The heart, he knew, hangs suspended in the chest . . . except when the patient is lying on his back. In the supine position the heart rests against the aorta. If the patient were propped up to a sitting position, might not the heart hang lower? And might that not reveal the ballooning aorta?

It was a simple thing to do, and he tried it.

It worked.

The area in the center of the chest, between the lungs, is known as the mediastinum and contains the heart and the aorta. In the normal trauma patient the upright X ray showed the heart low in the center of the chest and the big aorta silhouetted fuzzily above it. When the aorta was ruptured, the shadow was wider. Much wider. An amateur could tell the difference.

The X-ray technician's finger outlines the shadow of the policeman's widened mediastinum. "All ruptured aortas show a widened mediastinum," she tells the student. "Sometimes the patient is normal, which is why they have to take them up for an aortagram. It's worth an occasional fire drill, because mostly it's accurate."

Before his third heart attack killed him, Dr. Ayella saw the trauma unit become the only place in the world that routinely saves patients with ruptured aortas.

28

SOMETIMES IN MARCH, DARK GRAY CLOUDS BOIL across the Maryland countryside, bringing torrential rains and heavy thunder. The rain hammers loudly against the red brick facade of the sprawling medical school complex, but only the occasional sound of thunder penetrates into cubicle two, where the nurse trainee stands at the counter and immerses a strip of test paper in a small vial of urine. The color reassuringly changes from tan to blue.

Behind her, the alabaster man lies still in a CCRU bed. His blond head is suspended in a stainless steel cage that rests against a stack of pillows and is supported by his shoulders. The head is held in place in the center of the cage by rods attached to screws that are driven into the skull. The cage is designed to keep the hangman's fracture from shifting.

The patient's body is clothed in pajamas, a rarity on the trauma unit, and it lies very still, except for the regular rise and fall of the chest. But inside the cage the lips are active, moving soundlessly. There is no air for the vocal cords. Dials jump on the Engstrom respirator.

The urine test completed, the nurse trainee turns to check the intravenous flow and sees the moving lips. Concentrating, she bends over the face. Her eyes avoid his, focusing on the lips.

"Water," the lips say.

The nurse reaches for a half-filled glass with a bent hospital straw and moves it into range of the lips. The lips close around the straw and suck, while the eyes watch the face of the nurse. The nurse watches the water level fall, and when the sucking ceases she replaces the glass on the shelf.

"I'm going to be gone for a few minutes," the trainee says to the patient. Her voice is bright and artificial. The patient's eyes close tightly, and when they open again, the woman is gone.

Across the unit, Freckles breaks open a package containing a long, flexible tube. The tubing attaches to the suction hose and the nurse's left hand pops the boy's respirator tube off. The squat little machine on the far side of the bed begins to beep insistently.

Freckles snakes the tube quickly through the plastic tracheostomy aperture and deep into the boy's lungs. There is a loud slurping sound and yellow liquid fills the tube, traveling toward the Dispolex. Larry's cough reflex does not function. When the slurping stops, the tube is quickly withdrawn and deposited in the trash can. Reconnected, the respirator ceases to beep.

In the adjacent cubicle, a loud alarm goes off as Walter attempts to change position. He's more active now, which makes him more trouble.

"Got that," Freckles calls to the other nurses as she walks over to shut off the alarm. The monitors can't distinguish between a sudden fall in blood pressure and an impatient jostling of sensors.

At the opposite end of the unit, the face in the metal cage stares calmly upward as the sounds of Shocktrauma enter his ears. The respirator murmurs softly and somewhere a transformer buzzes. Glass clicks against metal, and an X-ray machine whines past on heavy rubber tires. Voices emerge from the background noise, only to disappear again. "No, Walter, not that one, this one. ... The orders say every hour, but I'm doing it more often because the lab says ... Institute for Emergency Medicine, may I help you ... *Dr. Cowley, 6846, Dr. Cowley, 6846 ...*"

From inside the cage, the blue pupils lock into focus. The lips move urgently. They are difficult to read, so the face repeats the words several times.

"Is ... it ... raining ... ?" the lips say. *"Hear ... thunder."* The expression is intent. Behind the patient, numbers move across the face of an electronic display and the heart signal bounces across the screen. The lips move on.

"I ... can't ... move. Ever."

Muffled thunder penetrates the unit, and the lights flicker briefly as the hospital's auxiliary power cuts in. From the far corner of the unit, a slurping sound is followed by a burst of short, anguished coughs.

"It ... hurts ..." say the lips.

The dry voice box clicks with each pantomimed word. The eyes fill with tears.

"Turn ... me. ... off. ..." the lips say. *"Please ..."*

218

A few yards away, in the nurses' lounge, a tall city policeman with a bushy mustache and hair slightly longer than regulations allow looks up briefly when the nurse trainee walks into the room and checks her mail pigeonhole. The man's eyes watch her as she walks down the hallway toward the nurse-chairman's office. Then the policeman resumes his studying.

The nurse trainee taps lightly on the nurse-chairman's door, then opens it partway. "Can I see you for a minute? It's important. . . . "

Around the corner in the CCRU, Freckles pushes a hypodermic needle through the rubber top of a vial and withdraws a small amount of Pavulon, the curare-like substance that was earlier used to paralyze the tetanus patient in cubicle one. Setting the vial aside, she turns and injects the paralyzing drug into a hanging bag of dextrose and saline.

Paralytic drugs like Pavulon are used by spiders and wasps to preserve prey, insects meant to feed their future offspring. South American natives rub their arrowheads in it to relieve themselves from the chore of tracking wounded animals. Penetrated by a curare-smeared arrow, the deer or agouti continues for a moment to think and feel, but loses its ability to act. The stricken animal's brain commands the legs to run and the diaphragm to breathe, but the muscles don't respond. Suffocation is rapid. Pavulon forces its way into the junctions between muscles and nerves, severing communication. It is a useful drug in Shocktrauma.

Larry was a fighter, and he probably would have exhausted himself. Tex and Freckles agreed on that. As consciousness returned, his mouth worked constantly, saying nothing that anybody could decipher. The weakened body lunged against the restraints, and the sewn-up diaphragm fought the rhythm of the Engstrom. The alarms sounded frequently as the thrashing disturbed the monitor lines, and once Larry even managed to rip the tube from his left forearm. The nurses had begun to worry that they might miss something in all the commotion. Tex hadn't wanted to use higher doses of morphine. In the first place, he didn't want Larry to become an addict and, in the second place, the nervous system was already injured by shock. Drugnumbed cells are slow to repair themselves.

But by far the most important factor in the decision was the energy that Larry couldn't afford to use up in useless fight. Larry's enemy was infection and death, not Freckles.

When his heart stopped, Freckles kept his brain from suffocating. When the bleeding in his abdomen threatened to outpace the drip of the transfusion bags, Tex repeatedly saved his life. When his kidneys temporarily failed, the dialysis technician, using techniques developed especially for trauma patients, rescued him again. On a minute-to-minute basis in the CCRU, Freckles now controls the metabolism that is unable to tune itself, and each adjustment is lifesaving.

The shock injured every cell in Larry's body, and it is crucial that the energy that could go toward rebuilding damaged tissue, not be squandered on fighting . . . or even respiration. Were is not for the Engstrom, breathing alone would consume fourteen percent of Larry's strength. Fighting would take it all.

Larry's second-crisis hours are made even more dangerous by the nature of his principal wound. Most people can get along well on a fragment of liver. But Larry is sick, and so is what remains of his liver.

Ironically, in the days before the trauma unit, the liver was considered almost impervious to shock. The misperception turned out to be a replay of the now-old story. Doctors hadn't seen shock-damaged livers because motorists with injuries that severe were being taken to the nearest hospitals, and from there, directly to the morgue.

When such a rare patient didn't die, the shocked-liver syndrome wasn't recognized because the liver is a very complex organ and because, in the nature of things, the doctors who stood around the bed had never seen a case quite like that before.

Larry's liver, when it was functioning properly, served a bewildering number of functions. It snapped up toxins and pollutants from the passing blood and changed their chemical structures, rendering them harmless. Thick growths of hunter-killer cells lined its tiny blood channels, devouring bacteria, viruses and odd chunks of garbage. Hormones were pulled in and destroyed so that the body's chemical communications system wasn't disrupted by background "noise." Nutrients were changed into more efficient forms. And on a molecular level, the organ performed thousands of critical but small chemical alterations to the specifications of other organs. Now the liver is doing none of these things well. Some it is not doing at all.

While the patient's individual cells struggle to repair the shock damage and get rid of the broken parts, the local garbage dump, pollution-control, tool-making and repair departments are, themselves, closed for repairs. The colony of cells that composes Freckles's patient teeters at the brink of chaos.

Freckles and Tex can't repair the injured liver cells, and there is no artificial liver similar to the kidney machine. But what the trauma team can do is minimize the biochemical damage to the rest of the body and, if everything else scrapes through, the liver will repair itself. But if bacteria gain a foothold in the defenseless colony, or if the heart stops, the liver will never have the opportunity.

Freckles's job is a grueling one. She moves around the bed, performing on-the-spot damage control, handling crises, watching the dials, administering drugs, adjusting the respirator and hanging bottles of liquid in anticipation of oscillations that, with skill, will not develop. She calls for dialysis and contacts Tex for strategic decisions, seeking the perfection that will keep Larry alive yet one more eight-hour shift. Her voice talks to his disconnected mind in soothing, motherly tones, but her brain processes data, evaluates the odds and fights the little things that could kill him.

But as Larry's primary nurse, Freckles's most overriding concern is that she might save the patient only to see him lose himself. What is his mind doing? Freckles talks aloud to him about a book she once read, *Desirée*, that dealt with the Napoleonic era. Does that strike his historical interest? She asks his mother about the cocker spaniels, and reports to him daily on their continued good health. Does he care? All she knows for certain is that he feels pain. Pain makes the dot on the heart monitor jump furiously. Freckles turns away from the island, opens a package of antacid tablets and discreetly slips two of the white pills between her teeth.

Each time she leaves the cubicle, she assures Larry that she'll be right back. Today, she has had to leave frequently as she prepares Walter for transfer out of the CCRU. A patient with gangrene is on his way to the unit, and there are no empty cubicles. Walter, being nearer recovery than any of the other patients, is being triaged out.

It is difficult for a trauma nurse not to identify with any but the most abusive patient, and there had been a special sympathy for the bungling stick-up artist whose plight was so starkly illustrated by the uniformed man in the lounge. The impending transfer to the main hospital's prison wing had a depressing effect on everyone, including Walter.

After he learned of the decision to transfer him out, Walter's psychological outlook deteriorated rapidly. Twice in the last hour he has asked for morphine. Left alone in his cubicle, while Freckles tends Larry, he writhes and turns, constantly setting off alarms. Freckles stands at the foot of his bed and gives the cubicle one last check. Walter is ready. She returns to the more critical of her two patients.

Freckles doesn't know what she'll do when Larry comes off the Pavulon and asks about Linda. He will have had time to think, and this time the question will probably be impossible to evade. While waiting in the lounge this morning before shift change, Freckles discussed the situation with two other CCRU nurses. One said she'd tell the patient, no matter what the family said. The other said she wouldn't, not if she could avoid it. It sometimes seems odd, but families often know best.

Not always, though, Freckles had reminded her. Remember the disc jockey disaster? The man who was given curare, and his wife said he liked to listen to a certain popular radio station because his clock radio was turned to it, and it woke him up every morning?

The nurse laughs. Everybody remembers that one. The primary nurse had brought in her own radio and set it up beside the man's bed, and played the same station all day, every day, for a week. Finally, the patient came off curare. The first thing he did was beg them to turn the radio off. He hated the station. Passionately. He used it for his clock radio because it helped remind him of the inane world he was going to have to crawl out of bed and deal with.

It was a pleasant conversation, but not very helpful to Freckles. Maybe she will just wait for Larry to ask, and then react in whatever way feels best.

Now, as she drops artificial tears into his half-open eyes, she stands a moment longer than necessary, stroking Larry's thick black hair, talking. Her voice is calm and reassuring, but her pulse rate is higher than her patient's. She'll do what she must.

Later, after she has given Larry a painkiller and the heart rate is slow, the beat that accompanies sleep, she leaves for a cigarette in the rest room. She takes the long way out of the CCRU, stopping to stand in front of cubicle three, where Linda lies beneath the extended arm of the Engstrom. Freckles does not cross the red line. Linda is not her patient and Freckles has never volunteered to care for her.

There was a time when Freckles would have automatically crossed the line, opened the record and hungrily devoured its contents. It made her a better primary nurse for a while and then . . . she quit doing it. Knowing her own patients absorbed all her energies. She didn't need to cross the line. The parents didn't want to talk about it, and that was fine with Freckles.

She knew enough . . . too much . . . from the unavoidably overheard conversations. They had taken Linda to some local hospital and her spleen was bleeding and they missed it. It busted loose late at night and everybody panicked, and they finally sent her to Shocktrauma. Too late. Standard story.

Freckles stands at the red line and looks at Linda from a distance.

They missed it.

"People die with little things," Cowley keeps saying. "They don't die with catastrophes. It was a little thing and somebody didn't notice, in the heat of the battle, and when you see the result of the oversight it's too late.

"It's *time*. I can go out and get money, and I can hire doctors. I can hire nurses. I can get helicopters and build a system and I can buy monitors, and equipment, and computers, but I can't buy time. I can't buy back that golden hour."

Now, in cubicle three, Linda's chest rises and falls at the bidding of the respirator. Fluid drops into her left wrist, but no urine collects in the plastic bag beneath the bed. Above her, the moving dot jumps and skips as it crosses the screen.

The colony of cells fought back, but too many were

225

damaged. Dialysis took the place of her nonfunctioning kidneys but there was nothing to be done about the dying liver. Antibiotics rarely work when there's nothing left of the immune system, and the bacteria came despite all the nurses could do.

As the days passed, Linda's skin turned an ominous yellow from the liver failure and the kidneys did not recover. A textbook collection of bacteria swam in her blood, and the relentless fever burned out her brain. In the small dimples where intravenous needles penetrate her flesh, droplets of pus collect. There is an unpleasant odor. Freckles turns away suddenly, her right hand fishing for the package of cigarettes in her pocket.

Out in the hallway near SYSCOM, the nurse-chairman's door opens slowly. The nurse trainee stands in the doorway for a moment. "I know," she says, "but it's what I want. I've thought about it." She closes the door as she leaves.

The policeman has put aside his textbook and now stands in the hallway by the lounge door. "Keep an eye on my prisoner," he says, as she approaches.

"He's not going anywhere," the trainee says.

The smile changes to a grin, and the policeman's right hand unconsciously caresses his service revolver. "Jeez, I wish he'd try."

The trainee stops instantly, her expression turning savage. "You'd like to shoot somebody, wouldn't you?" she snarls at the man, her fingers curling. "I bet you'd just dearly love to shoot somebody. Why don't you go on in and shoot the poor man with the broken neck? I bet that'd make you feel like a man, wouldn't it?"

Bafflement on his face, the policeman watches the nurse as she disappears into the unit. Finally, he shrugs.

In cubicle two, the trainee goes directly to the head in the cage. The eyes are closed. The heartbeat bounces steadily across the monitor screen and the dials all read normal. The nurse turns and opens the metal patient folder. There is a new entry on the current page, signed by a senior surgeon.

If the alabaster man begins to die, it instructs, "Do not resuscitate."

29

THE NEW PATIENT LIES ON THE FIRST AREA TA-
ble, conscious but sick. The doctors and nurses remove
the other hospital's lines and bandages while the team
leader reads the charts. The forty-five-year-old farmer
crushed his right wrist ten days ago, while removing a
tractor crankcase. At the hospital, the wounds were
cleaned, the bones pinned together and a cast put on.
Eventually the man went home from the hospital, but
returned three days later, feverish, seriously ill. There
was an unpleasant odor coming from the cast.

The organism that causes gas gangrene is one of medicine's stranger enemies. Most forms of life need oxygen
to survive but *Clostridium perfringens* uses the primitive
biochemical processes of the ancient seas. Its natural
environment contained no oxygen, and that gas is a
poison to it today.

The bacteria thrive on carrion, where there is flesh
but no oxygen-carrying blood, and like its relative that
causes tetanus, it usually lives in the soil. But *C. per-*

fringens can also consume live flesh with impaired circulation.

Once established, the gas gangrene organism secretes a toxin that turns the flesh around it into a frothy goo, which becomes the perfect habitat for the next generation of *C. perfringens*. The infection spreads through the muscle at a rate of several inches an hour and the poisons spread into the bloodstream. The patient becomes acutely ill.

Carefully, the team leader examines the wrist and hand. The tissue between thumb and wrist has sloughed away, and gas-filled bubbles crawl across the discolored palm. Antibiotic drugs are useless against *C. perfringens*, and the standard therapy is removal of the arm.

In the ages before surgeons learned to scrape away injured tissue, a process called debridement, gangrene was war's worst killer. It stalked the battlefield, claiming those with musket ball wounds of the leg or shell-fractured hands. A small sabre cut led to gas gangrene, and that led to amputation without anesthesia. Gas gangrene meant pain . . . and it still does.

Tex scrapes at the tissue with a sterile instrument, and the skin pulls away like clay. He scrapes deeper, depositing the gassy meat in a small stainless steel bowl. Unnecessary personnel drift away as the smell of rotting meat pervades the room. Tex scrapes again, and again and again.

Suddenly the farmer screams. It is a long, piercing howl, the sound of an animal.

Tex can't anesthetize him. The screams are the only way he can tell he's hit live flesh.

Downstairs, in the chamber room, an ex-Navy diver presses the requisition form against the metal side of the long, cylindrical pressure chamber. He signs his name boldly, hands the completed form to the waiting attendant and walks back along the long pressure chamber toward the control panel. Near the center of the chamber, a heavy steel door stands open to admit the gangrene patient.

The hyperbaric—high pressure—chamber was an early Cowley gamble, and for many years it was widely acknowledged by almost everyone but Cowley that the hunch had been wrong.

The idea grew naturally out of Cowley's theory that lack of oxygen perfusion was fundamental to shock, and that increasing oxygen perfusion in a shock patient should therefore make him better. He knew that many biochemical processes were going haywire in shocky tissue, but the suffocation was probably most important. After all, oxygen is the only thing that cells can't store.

The theory dovetailed nicely with the scientific facts about high-pressure therapy. At high pressures, gases dissolve more easily in liquids. At a pressure of forty-five pounds per square inch, three times the normal atmospheric pressure, a person breathing pure oxygen doesn't even need red blood cells to survive—enough oxygen dissolves in the clear plasma to keep the cells well-perfused and alive. It was obvious to Cowley that shock patients, who desperately need oxygen, would benefit from repeated dives in a hyperbaric chamber.

The idea offered special hazards, though. At three atmospheres of ordinary air, even asbestos will burn

. . . and so, for that matter, will human skin. At three atmospheres, the metal magnesium will burst into flame. Some metals, like mercury and beryllium, will evaporate, poisoning the air. Wrist watches, fountain pens, test tubes and medication bottles can be crushed by the pressure. The farmer's clothing is cut away and he's transferred to a specially prepared bed. There can be no nylon. Shoes with metal caps might strike a spark, and they're forbidden.

But the most important precaution is the trained diver who now checks the dials on the big floor-to-ceiling instrument board that rises beside the long pressure cylinder. No one but the retired Navy petty officers are allowed to supervise a dive and the manual makes it clear: They, not the doctor, are in charge.

In the beginning, Cowley had hoped that patients in shock would benefit dramatically from repeated dives in the chamber. But the results were, at best, equivocal.

The first dramatic advantage of the pressure chamber turned out to be its ability to supercharge gangrene-infected tissue with oxygen. And oxygen, of course, is deadly poison to *C. perfringens*. Many physicians heard about Cowley's success with gas gangrene long before they identified his name with trauma medicine.

Those were hard times for the Cowley team, when Shocktrauma had not yet gained its wide reputation for saving lives. Cowley's doctors, weary of unfavorable comparisons with Johns Hopkins in Baltimore, and Georgetown and George Washington in nearby D.C., made the most of the success. Dr. Boyd was probably the loudest, and he still tells the story with relish.

"We had a gas case flown in by the Navy, and that

got on television. Then we had about seven gas cases in a couple of weeks.

"We had one guy who was sick as hell and Hopkins sent him over here. Hopkins! Man, did that piss them off, for Hopkins to have to send a case over here!

"We took care of this guy, cleared up the gas and I personally took him back to Hopkins and tooted our goddamned horn to anybody I could find." Dr. Boyd pushed the recovered patient through the dignified hospital calling, "Returning a patient from the University of Maryland Shocktrauma unit . . . Returning a patient from the University of Maryland Shocktrauma unit . . . Returning a . . ."

Gas gangrene, which Cowley still considers one of the most treacherous problems in medicine, responded readily at the trauma unit. It was especially significant that the trauma unit, unlike most hospital facilities, was open and manned twenty-four hours a day.

"Gas gangrene is rapidly fatal," Cowley says. "In forty-eight hours you're dead, so it's got to be treated right now.

"I remember a boy who injured the top of his foot when he was fishing. First there was a big dark spot, and then the next thing he knew he had gas gangrene bubbles going up his leg. They tried to control it but couldn't, so they called in an orthopedic surgeon to do a mid-thigh amputation.

"But somebody said, 'Let's get him over to the chamber,' and so he wound up here and we dived him. Now he's cured, and he kept his leg.

"Gas gangrene is treatable. The oxygen kills the *C.*

perfringens the way hydrogen peroxide will kill certain bacteria."

The chamber also proved life-saving to people with carbon monoxide poisoning. The high-pressure oxygen drives the carbon monoxide out of their blood so rapidly that people dying after exhaust-fume poisoning would often wake up right in the chamber. Sometimes, when the patient is heavily laden with carbon monoxide, the fumes escaping from the body will make the dive team noticeably drowsy.

Cowley had his usual trouble convincing the local hospitals that they should send him their carbon monoxide patients. The price of that reluctance was dramatically illustrated by a luckless couple who went to sleep in a parked car with the engine running.

Both patients were rushed to the nearest hospital, where the emergency room staff decided that the woman could be treated in their hospital. But the man, who seemed much worse, was forwarded to Cowley. He woke up in the chamber. The woman died.

High-pressure oxygen was also used to treat an odd variety of problems including bone infections, certain types of cancer and radiation burns. The chamber is in use almost daily, but generally not for trauma patients. That unhappy fact has irritated Cowley for years.

But Cowley's hunches are seldom one hundred percent wrong, and recent research in Scotland suggests that the gamble may be useful in the treatment of severe spinal cord bruises which, today, are uniformly crippling.

A hangman's fracture remains irreversibly lethal, but if the cord is only bruised, not destroyed, the high pressure oxygen may keep the swelling nerves, which are encased in the vertebrae, from dying of suffocation. As usual in trauma medicine, though, the research indicates that the dive must be made fast . . . probably within the first four hours after the accident.

In the chamber room the technician clamps on a headset as the admitting team rolls the gangrene patient, now anesthetized, through the hatch. The hatches close heavily and are dogged from the inside. Standing outside, in front of the instrument board, the diver's hand touches a switch. From within the chamber comes the sound of rushing air.

30

AS THE SHIFT PROGRESSES AND THEY HAVE TIME,
the nurses prepare the cubicles. Sheets are draped
neatly over Christine's torso and her arms are placed
at her sides on top of the sheet. The urine bag is emptied, and a nurse experiments briefly in an attempt to
conceal the sensor in the top of her bald head with a
towel, but it doesn't work and she abandons the idea.
The attendants break out four tubular metal folding
screens and lean them against the island. Later they
will erect them to form a shielded walkway between the
CCRU entrance and bed ten.

At about noon a kidney specialist from the university
throws a pink gown over his tall form and strides quickly
into the CCRU, his short-legged female assistant rushing to keep up. The doctor walks directly to Christine's
cubicle and reaches for her chart without looking. As
he has told the patient's father this morning, there is
no Christine. The nephrologist flips open the record,
examines it and says something to his assistant. The
assistant writes in a notebook.

Finished there, the kidney specialist moves to the next bed, where Tommy lies with his head still in a white turban. Again the doctor checks the record and his assistant writes down his instructions.

A nurse reports to the doctor, smiling. The physician points to Tommy, then to Christine. The nurse nods affirmatively. The attendants begin erecting the screens.

Tommy's family waits in the nurses' lounge. There is a large, middle-aged woman in a black dress, an expressionless man in an inexpensive suit, a teenaged girl with a department store tape recorder, a younger boy, a priest and, sitting uncomfortably in a far corner, the team leader.

"I just wish we could have come sooner," the mother is saying, again.

"The doctor explained that," the priest says in a reassuring voice. "We tried to explain the risk of infection to you. But you're here now."

The team leader watches the human traffic as it passes the door, and when he sees the kidney doctor and his assistant pass, he rises and beckons for the family to follow. Outside, everybody puts on pink wraparounds and paper caps.

As they enter the unit, the team leader steps aside and the priest walks ahead of the family, through the corridor of white screens. An alarm sounds at the far end of the room and there is a subdued, "I got it" cry from a nurse.

The priest stops at the foot of the bed. The parents come next, the mother leaning on the father, and then the children.

Without warning, the woman shrieks, tears away

from her husband, evades a waiting trauma nurse and throws her arms around Tommy's neck. Overhead the dials swing erratically, the alarm light flashes and the respirator, suddenly disconnected, beeps plaintively. The mother leaps back in surprise.

As the nurse reconnects the respirator and the alarm stops, the mother approaches again and touches the boy more carefully. Her voice is loud and shrill. "Itsy Tommy hurt?

"We love you, Tommy. Barbara would have come but they wouldn't let her, and she sends her love and you're going to be all right, Tommy. . . . "

The youngest brother stands beside the bed. His gaze is fixed on Tommy's face, and his eyes are wide, staring, not blinking, his face as blank as the patient's. The girl stands with the priest, and tears run down her cheeks. Her mouth forms the words, "I didn't know." The priest touches her, but she moves away. Her fingers fiddle with the dials of the tape recorder. She holds the instrument up and looks at it, her face contorted.

Her mother calls her to the bedside, and she hesitates. The priest urges her forward and she walks, stiffly. There is a whispered conversation between the girl and her mother, the girl shaking her head, no, no, no. The mother lunges for the tape recorder and the girl steps backward.

"All right," the girl says. "If it's got to be done, I can do it."

She lays the tape recorder near Tommy's right ear and pushes the button. The volume is loud.

"Hello Tommy," the speaker says in a masculine voice. "Sorry I couldn't come to see you. Sounds like you got yourself in a bash, kid. Hurry up and get the hell out of there so we can go fishin', huh?"

There is a pause in the tape, and then the voice is feminine. "I'm not used to talking into one of these things, Tommy, but I know you'll be okay and . . ."

As the tape recorder continues, Tommy's chest rises and falls rhythmically. The three dots move, bouncing, across the screen. The dials read normal.

Tommy's nurse moves away, ducks between two folding screens, and climbs the island for a package of supplies. On the island, the clerk is staring, transfixed, at the scene below.

"The mother has no conception," the nurse whispers to the clerk, as the tape recorder shifts to a blaring pop tune. "That's his favorite goddamned song."

When the song ends the girl bolts, bawling, down the aisle between the screens. The brother, who had reached out to touch Tommy's arm, jerks his hand back without making contact. Slowly, the rest of the group disengages and moves away from the bed. The mother bursts into tears as the priest supports her back across the red line. She cries, "Tommy, Tommy, Tommy."

The kidney specialist approaches the family in the hallway outside SYSCOM. Again he asks the question, softly, urgently.

"No," the father says, his arm around his wife's shoulder. "Just no. Leave us alone."

"Don't hurt him any more," the mother adds. "You've hurt him enough."

A black woman mopping the hallway nearby stops and turns around, curious. The kidney specialist looks at the team leader. The team leader looks back and shrugs.

"You're wrong," the kidney man says to the mother. "We haven't hurt him at all, and nobody can hurt him now."

But the mother, crying on her husband's shoulder, isn't listening. The elevator door is open and they are soon aboard, and the door closes. The kidney specialist licks his lips and, removing the paper cap, runs his right hand through his thin hair. There is no appeal. Out in the CCRU, the attendants are rearranging the screens.

The second family is more subdued. The man and woman arrive alone, and they stand together for a long time at the foot of Christine's bed. Finally, the mother walks over and kisses the girl on the left cheek, then returns to bury her own cheek against the pink gown that covers her husband's paint-flecked working jacket.

The man puts his arms around the woman, but his eyes don't leave the small body. His eyes are dark and baggy, and there are scabs on his heavy knuckles.

They leave as quietly as they came, and the kidney specialist watches them from the island. There are no words exchanged now. The words were said earlier.

"Someone, somewhere should benefit," the mother had said.

31

___

ONCE AGAIN TEX STANDS IN CUBICLE NUMBER three and reads from Linda's medical record. Numbers and chemical names record her steady and predictable disintegration. Her immune system gone, the bacteria *Escherichia coli*, which are normally harmless denizens of the bowel, swim in company with her red blood cells. Their excretions poison the muscular arterial walls, which relax and dilate. The blood pressure falls. Each day her skin turns yellower as whole communities of dying cells spew out poisons that the liver can't remove.

Tex snaps the record shut with excessive force. The morning of Linda's admission, Tex had examined her thoroughly, and then he got on the phone to the emergency room physician who had treated her and sent her to him. He called the surgeon a lot of things, but the worst thing that he called him was an ignorant quack, and he knew as soon as he hung up the telephone that he shouldn't have done it. At least that's what he told the senior traumatologist who called him at home six hours later and invited him downtown for a chat. The words the man had used most often and most loudly were, "You can't do that."

Medical lore has it that you can spot a psychiatrist by the shape of his beard, a surgeon by his swagger and a pediatrician by a certain juvenile look. Similarly, trauma specialists are noted for their big mouths.

Cowley, for instance, always picked the most inopportune times to suggest that people were dying unnecessarily. They wouldn't die so often, he argued, if the state had an adequate system. The ambulance squads should cooperate with the police and with the emergency rooms, and the basis of that cooperation should be the well-being of the patient ... and not the politics of the ambulance companies, the jealousies of the hospitals or the economics of mandatory liability insurance.

Cowley spread those notions during what was already an awkward era for the medical profession. As doctors became less accessible and emergency room waiting areas became more crowded, prices soared and the quality of medical care plummeted so dramatically that even the lay public knew it.

In direct response to public dissatisfaction, the federal government had moved to remedy matters by taking the medical profession in hand. The vehicles of control were to be regional planning organizations, which were sprouting up across the bureaucratic countryside. There was even talk that the councils might start telling individual hospitals which services they could provide and which they could not.

Statistics had shown that large, busy heart surgery

suites, for example, had better survival rates than small, less busy ones . . . presumably because the busiest teams got the most experience. Now the public was beginning to demand to know which hospitals were successful with what kinds of treatments and which weren't.

The issue was an explosive one. The medical societies and hospital associations stood four-square against any such disclosure, and a confrontation seemed inevitable. And now, to make matters worse, this loudmouth heart surgeon was saying inflamatory things about emergency rooms. And he was saying them to reporters, and they were true.

A group of Baltimore emergency room physicians began meeting Saturday mornings to talk about the situation. The group called itself Med-Heads, and it was composed of men whose perspectives on medicine generally differed dramatically from Cowley's.

Med-Heads' founder, the assistant chief medical officer for Baltimore city, often invited representatives of the press and the political establishment to attend the breakfast meetings.

One such guest was Frederick L. Dewberry, an influential Democrat. "You know," he says, remembering the emergency room doctors, "each one of them . . . all of a sudden they'd start making speeches about their own particular area of medicine. All they talked about were their own special interests. It was quite evident, the opposition and the feeling about Cowley."

On the record, Med-Heads doctors deflected questions about Cowley, but in private they were blunt. "Cowley is an egotistical, power-happy, empire-building son of a bitch," snarled one aged, long-toothed man who ran a local emergency room program.

The Med-Heads president had guessed right when he invited Dewberry to that Saturday morning meeting, because the Democrat was soon appointed to head the governmental panel that many, Cowley included, hoped would put the medical house in order. The committee's charter made it responsible for coordinating the growth of health services throughout the region.

In theory, since traffic accidents don't respect jurisdictional boundaries, the group would have a large hand in the establishment of a new and badly needed emergency medical system. But in fact, the large committee of doctors was hamstrung by the desire of the medical community to alter the status quo as little as possible. Cowley had a seat on the panel, but his was a lonely voice.

"Dr. Cowley," says Dewberry, "is a strong personality and he knows how to get things done. He's a damn good administrator and he's a good politician. He's good all around, you see, which puts him quite a few steps ahead of his colleagues in the medical profession. They take umbrage at this, unfortunately."

At the time, the federal government had just announced that it would give grants of four million dollars each to five regions willing to develop area-wide emergency care systems. The Baltimore committee decided to try for the money, which meant a regional plan had to be developed, and quickly. They had to tell the government what they expected to spend the money on.

Cowley, of course, offered his plan as a model. It was rejected. When the regional plan finally emerged from a series of committee meetings, it was a monument to group-think and respect for territory. The proposed scheme of emergency care remained based on the nearest-hospital approach, and Baltimore didn't get the money.

One of the winners was Illinois, with a proposal written by a bright young trauma doctor named David Boyd. Boyd's proposal bore a striking resemblance to the one Cowley had urged in Baltimore.

But, as Cowley argued, research scientists began making his points for him. Perfusion was, in fact, the key to shock. The golden hour was real. Shock lung could be stopped.

But within Baltimore's medico-political climate, the most telling scientific report of all was one written by a woman who was also, like Cowley, addicted to numbers. Her name was Susan P. Baker, an internationally-known Johns Hopkins health statistician and epidemiologist. Her paper, published in the *Journal of Trauma,* gave Cowley the ammunition he needed.

Ms. Baker had checked through the autopsy records of traffic victims who, according to the state medical examiner, had died of internal bleeding. Fully one-third of them could have been saved, she concluded, if they had been diagnosed earlier. There was, of course, only one way to make the diagnosis earlier, and that was the controversial belly tap.

If Cowley the loudmouth grated on his colleagues' nerves, Cowley with numbers was downright insufferable, an incendiary. Doctors stopped criticizing his medicine and focused more on Cowley the man.

And that was the atmosphere when a new dean took over the University of Maryland medical school.

Dr. John H. Moxley III was a thirty-five-year-old academic physician fresh from Harvard, and he was welcomed as a bright young symbol of a new era. A man like that, it was said, could bring in fresh new minds to infuse the medical school with the vigor it so sadly lacked.

Almost immediately, Dr. Moxley had an opportunity to do just that. The chief of surgery died in an automobile accident in France. His successor would be Cowley's boss . . . if anyone could be said to boss Cowley.

Dr. Moxley's sights finally settled on Dr. G. Robert Mason, a respected surgeon from Stanford who shared Cowley's interest in the field of traumatology. Without consulting Cowley, Moxley said later, he effectively used the Shocktrauma unit to entice Dr. Mason to Baltimore.

Dr. Moxley didn't worry too much about Cowley because, as he saw it, the combative heart surgeon was only intimidating by comparison. "Look at the people around him!" the dean would later recall. "You had to have forceful people around him, but we had nobody."

Now, however, he had Dr. Mason.

The new chief of surgery was tall and strikingly handsome, a cultured and articulate man who used words like "quaternary" in ordinary conversation. He was a gentleman who nodded encouragingly as he listened to opposing opinions, a man who believed strongly in the academic and medical processes, who trusted consensus and value consultations. Cowley, of course, was none of those things.

245

If Dr. Moxley had the taming of Cowley in mind when he selected Dr. Mason as chief of surgery, Dr. Mason doesn't remember being warned. He had to discover for himself the delicate and independent genius brooding in the trauma unit.

Doctors Mason and Cowley apparently agreed that the state needed a coordinated emergency medical network, and they agreed that the best such network would be centered at University Hospital. But Cowley had already begun to act, and not by committee. He already had the system designed, and he showed it to any official who found time to listen, and to some who didn't.

One of the most circumspect was the state's health secretary, a diet-book author who looked at the thick sheaf of papers Cowley sent him and composed a polite reply. The secretary said the idea was interesting, and he suggested that Cowley try again later . . . say, in about six years.

Cowley also sent a copy of the plan to the governor, hoping Mandel would remember the days when Jim Mause was in the unit. But Cowley sent it through channels, and the governor never saw it.

Two of Cowley's supporters, a judge and a newspaper editor, suggested a more expeditious route. He should talk with a friend of the governor's, Frank A. DeFilippo, a dapper little fellow with slicked-back hair and, it is said, 200 fine suits. They assured Cowley that DeFilippo had the savvy to understand the Cowley dream and might even be willing to help.

DeFilippo had been a successful newspaper reporter back in the days when success meant getting the hell out of the business. He worked for the Baltimore *News-*

American, covering the state legislature in Annapolis. There, he became friendly with the diminutive, pipe-smoking Speaker of the House of Delegates, a man named Marvin Mandel. When Spiro Agnew resigned the governorship to accept the vice-presidency, Marvin Mandel was chosen to complete the term. Mandel asked DeFilippo to be his press secretary, and DeFilippo agreed.

DeFilippo delighted in politics as only an ex-reporter can. He had the governor's ear and used it. Before long, the governor sought and accepted his advice on matters great and small, down to his choice of suits. DeFilippo was a pipeline to the governor and was thus a contact for what he called "supplicants," people like Cowley who came to ask a favor.

DeFilippo liked the good life as much as he liked the power, and Friday nights often found him dining at a popular restaurant called Sabatino's. Sabatino's is the kind of place where Cadillacs park outside in the daytime. One Friday night, down at Sabby's, DeFilippo looked up from his plate to see the hulking form of R Adams Cowley.

"I had no idea who this guy was. I had never met him. Never heard of him. He said, in his very gentle way, 'I wonder if you'd have a minute, there's something I'd like to talk to you about.' So he lays this whole thing on me, right over dinner. And he lays it on me in such a way that if I don't do this and that, people are gonna die. Here's the street littered with corpses, and here I am having veal instead of doing something about it."

Cowley fascinated DeFilippo. The mess Cowley was

in fascinated him. The glimmer of medical politics . . .
Cowley talked and DeFilippo listened.

Cowley said he wanted to create a statewide emergency medical system, and make the trauma unit the
center of it. He explained what was happening on the
highways. He explained what a statewide system would
do about that. He presented his plan, and it sounded
sensible enough to DeFilippo. The way to do it, the
press secretary said, was to get the governor to sign an
executive order to that effect. Finally, Cowley let
DeFilippo eat his veal.

Cowley started going to Sabatino's every Friday
night. Naturally, he bumped into DeFilippo and, just
as naturally, he inquired into the health of the executive
order. After all, people were dying. Finally, DeFilippo
says, "I started badgering the governor about it, and I
got Cowley down there to talk to him, and one thing
led to another. . . . "

32

THE PAPERWORK IS COMPLETED BY LATE AFTER-
noon and a surgeon, a surgical resident, a nurse and a
technician from nephrology come for Christine. A
trauma nurse assists them in mobilizing the bed and
equipment and an anesthesiologist checks her respirator. The readings are perfect. The kidneys should be
in good condition.

In the adjacent cubicle, where Tommy lies, a hand
reaches out and flicks off the respirator. Abruptly, his
breathing stops but the heartbeat continues to bounce
across the monitor screen, sixty beats a minute. The
clock says 4:33 P.M.

A nurse stands nearby, writing in Tommy's patient
record, her eye occasionally going to the heartbeat signal, which continues strong, sixty beats a minute, sixty
beats a minute. As the minutes pass, the preparations
in Christine's cubicle cease. All eyes watch the moving
dot above Tommy's bed.

It is 4:34. The dot mesmerizes. Sixty beats a minute,
sixty beats a minute. The cells of the heart can't perform

their chemical function without oxygen, but the heart is a strong muscle. It beats on.

"It's a young heart," the anesthesiologist says.

On the dials, the blood pressure wavers and drops, recovers, and climbs slowly back to normal. The eyes watch the dot move across the screen.

Five minutes pass and the dials fall, hold and fall again.

"Pressure is 60," the nurse says.

Tommy lies motionless, eyes closed, liquids still dripping into his veins. The surgeon is drawn away from Christine's bed, toward the screen where the heartbeat is steady, sixty beats a minute, sixty beats a minute.

"Pressure is 50." Everyone stands silently. The clock turns.

"Hey," the surgeon says, breaking the spell. "Did you hear about the patient they had in here the other day? The one with the . . . this is true, go look it up . . . she had a fractured tit."

His eyes remain fixed on the bouncing dot.

"A what?" asks Tommy's nurse, blushing slightly. "You can't fracture that."

"Well, she did," says the surgeon. "She had one of those silicone implants to make her boobs bigger. And she was driving a Porsche with a loose shoulder belt. Popped the goddamned thing. Her left one was "C" cup and her right one was an "A." The guy down in Admitting went berserk, couldn't figure out what the hell was wrong with her until she told him."

"Poor lady," says the nurse.

Everybody watches the dot bounce across the screen, sixty beats a minute.

"Poor lady my ass," says the surgeon. "She liked the busted one better than the other one. In fact, the plastic surgeon went in her room the other day and popped the other one, so they'd look alike. The woman said they never looked right anyhow, and she liked them better popped."

"Pressure is 45."

The dot goes on and on, sixty beats a minute, sixty beats a minute. Tommy's chest does not move.

"It's definitely a case for the medical historians," says the resident. The second hand sweeps around twice, three times.

"Pressure is 40."

"A busted tit. Think of it. A busted tit."

"Pressure is 30."

"It's been known to take an hour," the surgeon says. "He was a young guy. His heart was fine. I wish we could do hearts."

"You can't even do his kidneys," the nurse says.

The heart beats on, sixty beats a minute, moving across the screen, the cells suffocating, poisonous wastes accumulating, shock deepening, but still beating on, sixty beats a minute, sixty beats a minute.

The heart skips a beat and, instantly, the alarm goes off. The nurse quickly moves to flip off the forgotten alarm system.

The heart recovers and the motion resumes, sixty beats a minute, sixty beats a minute.

"It's a shame," someone says, "that people are dying for want of a heart."

Suddenly the dot begins to transcribe a long, slow curve, a steady wave, an oscillation.

"What you're seeing," says the surgeon, "is a young heart dying."

The wavy line straightens and the dot bounces once, twice and then it beats again, sixty beats a minute, sixty beats a minute, sixty beats a minute.

The second hand sweeps around. The technician dries the palms of her hands by sliding them along the fabric of her pink gown. Not far away an attendant has put on another pot of coffee, and its perking clutters the silence, banging against the lid of the percolator. It perks more slowly than the heart beats, at first, but as the second hand sweeps around again and again, the pace of the perking increases. For a moment, it is in rhythm with the heartbeat, sixty beats a minute, sixty beats a minute. Then the coffee pot is faster.

"Goddamn," someone breathes. "It takes forever."

And then the bouncing stops, suddenly. There is no wave. Just a line, a moving line that begins on the left side of the screen and moves steadily across to disappear on the right.

The surgeon is the first to turn away, and then the team is back at Christine's bed, breaking connections, getting ready to roll. The anesthesiologist pops off the respirator tube and quickly replaces it with a large black bag which he squeezes to pump oxygen manually into the lungs. Christine's chest continues to rise and fall as the bed moves out and down the hall, toward the hospital's distant surgical suites. In the operating room the senior surgeon lets the resident make the single slice down the center of the girl's belly and remove the kidneys.

He takes them out with great care, one by one, and

the technician connects them to a small machine designed to perfuse them with chilled salt water. A driver waits outside to rush them to Baltimore-Washington International Airport, where two pilots are preflighting their aircraft. One kidney will go to Tennessee, where it will be transplanted into a mother of four and the other will go to Iowa, for a telephone lineman.

During the trip upstairs from the trauma unit and throughout the brief operation, the anesthesiologist monitored Christine's vital signs, supplied drugs to correct metabolic oscillations, and kept her lungs inflating. Now, when the second kidney is safely transferred to the travel device, he catches the surgeon's attention.

"You guys need me any more?" he asks.

"No," says the surgeon. "Thanks."

The anesthesiologist shuts down his machines and walks away.

33

FOR EIGHT DAYS, THE YOUNG INSURANCE EXECU-
tive with the hangman's fracture lies still in cubicle two.
The nurse trainee feeds him ice cream and pudding and,
when she has time, reads aloud from a paperback book
of short stories.

In midweek, a special exception is made and the patient's mother, father and pregnant wife are helped into
pink wraparounds and paper caps and allowed to stand
for a few minutes beside the bed. The mother insists
that "it'll all work out."

His wife stands silently, squeezing a lifeless hand.
Finally, holding the hand so the patient can see it, she
presses it briefly against her swollen belly. She leaves
without ever speaking a word.

The alabaster man sleeps frequently now, but only
until each dose of sedatives wears off. Often he hovers
on the edge of sleep for several minutes, eyes fluttering.
Then the lids snap back and the pupils dart frantically
across the sky of hanging bags and draped tubing above

him. Sometimes the nurse wipes away tears with small squares of gauze.

His temperature travels the unit's grapevine.

"It's up again," the trainee tells Freckles. "It might be tonight." Freckles tells the SYSCOM dispatcher and the dispatcher tells the admitting nurse. Soon the information is general knowledge.

Downstairs, on the second floor, Dr. McAslan explains that the diaphragm, which provides the sucking power for the lungs, operates according to nerve impulses that travel down from the brain, along the spinal cord.

If the cord is destroyed low in the neck, those pathways often survive, and then the patient can breathe on his own. Usually, in that case, he often has some control over his arms and hands as well. Such a patient can live a long and useful, though grotesquely limited, life as a quadriplegic.

But when the neck is broken just below the base of the skull, destroying the spinal cord, the victim will never breathe without a respirator. Dr. McAslan says his Engstroms can do wondrous things, but they are not as good as the natural respiration system and they cannot preserve life indefinitely.

The anesthesiologist says it is usually impossible to tell at the accident scene or in the admitting area whether the spinal cord is destroyed or merely bruised. Bruised spinal cords occasionally regain some function, so the doctors and nurses do what they can. But when the patient doesn't improve . . .

"Then it is a matter of unfortunate circumstances,

you see. You have a person who's mentally alert. He's able to hear and see. He can't talk, but he can hear and see . . . he can smile. He can cry. He's got all the emotions. He knows who you are, he knows his wife or child. He can see them and he can smile."

The irony is that the sophisticated trauma unit is one of the few places capable of keeping such a patient alive, and even there it can't be done indefinitely. Ultimately, deprived of the brain's orchestration, the body chemistry begins to go haywire. Oscillations begin, and widen. Infection sets in or the heart simply stops.

If the patient continues to live, he must eventually be transferred to another place. The trauma beds are needed for patients who can improve, so the quadriplegic is transferred to a nursing home or, if there is money available, to a specialized facility expert in the care of totally paralyzed people.

"Usually," says McAslan, "as soon as you remove them from the minute-to-minute care of a sophisticated environment, complications develop and these people die.

"Maintenance of a patient on a respirator is a very skilled business. It requires highly trained physicians and nurses around the clock. You need a whole team to take care of the lungs, to see that secretions are removed, to treat infections and body sores . . . you need constant attention. If you take that away, they don't live very long.

"You know you are sentencing that man to hell in many ways by keeping him alive, and you know that you're sentencing the family to hell."

Once, he says, when the need was clear, such patients

were removed from the respirator and allowed to die. When a *Washington Post* medical writer visited the unit, the trauma doctors discussed the procedures frankly, and their quotes were included in a series on euthanasia.

The ensuing uproar pitted the Shocktrauma team against the medical society, the hospital and the attorney general of Maryland. Shocktrauma lost. Now, euthanasia is no longer sanctioned at the unit.

Dr. Schnaper, the psychiatrist, was one of the doctors called on the carpet after the *Washington Post* articles. For a while, he said, he feared he might be charged with murder. "Now . . . it's a sad thing to watch. They look terrible, depressed, sometimes they linger on and on . . . you see tears."

The change in official policy resulted in a series of pacts between trauma team members. Nearly everyone who works at the unit has talked with someone he trusts, someone who, if need be, would come as a final friend. But there is no friend for the man with the hangman's fracture.

For eight days he lies in cubicle two. In the numb body, infection takes hold and the temperature soars, but the immune system is young and powerful, and it falls again. The brain behind the blue eyes sleeps, and wakes, and sleeps and wakes. The heart beats on and on.

Finally, the pregnant woman and the team leader spend a long time in the nurse-chairman's office with the door shut, and the next day two private ambulance attendants arrive to transfer the alabaster man to a nursing home.

The ambulance attendants are careful but they aren't

trained in the management of such delicate cases and, somehow, in the course of the transfer, bacteria colonize the urinary catheter. By the time it's discovered the infection has moved through the kidneys and into the bloodstream. Two days later the rising temperatures burn out the brain.

34

AS THE DAYS PASS, LARRY'S KIDNEYS SLOWLY improve until, finally, the dialysis machine is no longer needed. The slight yellow tinge fades from his skin and his brushes with sepsis become infrequent, then disappear.

When Tex and Freckles are convinced that Larry can no longer fatally exhaust himself, the paralyzing Pavulon is discontinued and, as movement returns, Freckles steels herself for the question.

But the first words she reads from the silent lips are about the pain. For days Larry hangs in a morphine fog, becoming more alert as the painkilling drugs are steadily decreased. He doesn't fight now and, while he communicates only infrequently with the nurses, he seems in good spirits. There is no question about Linda, no reference to her. It is as though she did not exist.

Freckles would have preferred to face the question.

As she explained to Tex, she'd made her peace with that one. She wouldn't lie. Period. Tex had provided the necessary assent by saying nothing.

Freckles was ready and Larry didn't ask, and the obvious explanation was that in the days he'd spent on Pavulon, locked in his skull, alone, with his guilt . . . he had chosen to reject the question and thereby avoid the answer. Now he was improving each day, and Freckles could leave him frequently to care for the farmer with gangrene. Soon he would move out to the intensive care overflow unit, and then he would see his parents. Before he moves out, Freckles will warn the primary nurse who will follow him through the rest of his stay in Shocktrauma.

This morning, Freckles has spent more than half her time treating the farmer. Though she wasn't his primary nurse, she is growing to like the man, who reminds her of the way her grandfather had been when she was young. The man in bed eight is strong and practical and, once he understood its necessity, he had learned to suffer silently the process of debridement. He simply shut his eyes and clenched his teeth. The doctor could tell when he hit live tissue by the hiss of air between his incisors.

The noise level is higher than usual in the unit this shift. Patients are being moved out.

The bustle in the CCRU is an echo of the controlled pandemonium down in the admitting area. Within the space of an hour and a half, four patients have arrived. A light plane crash produced three patients, but one of them arrested in Admitting and they couldn't get his heart started again. The other two are both in the operating rooms.

The fourth patient is a shipyard worker who fell into the hold of a cargo ship and has internal bleeding, plus broken bones. The second back-up team is preparing to take him into operating room one, where one of the airplane crash victims is undergoing surgery to remove a piece of metal beam from his pelvis. It is awkward to operate on two patients in the same OR, but it can be done.

Finally, a few minutes ago, the loud speaker announced that the helicopter is on its way with still another patient, this one from the shoulder of the John F. Kennedy Expressway. Pedestrian. Expressway pedestrians are always bad. Housekeeping is working frantically to clean the first admitting area before the aircraft lands. The nurses are walking on the wet floor to restock.

The scene upstairs is not yet frantic, just hurried. The wave won't hit the CCRU for hours yet. But when they start coming up from the operating rooms, they will need the womb's every service. And the CCRU is, at this moment, full. Triage has begun, and the most stable patients are prepared for transfer to the overflow unit.

The woman with tetanus is the first one to make the passage back across the red line. The therapy for tetanus is horrifying but the results are dramatic. Several days ago the trauma team eased up on the Pavulon, and the shaking was gone. The woman is still very weak, but after a few days in the overflow unit she will be ready to return to her husband . . . who will be able to visit her this evening for the first time since she was admitted. Death is not so close in the overflow unit and brief visits are allowed.

The next to go is the young electrician who almost died, his chest flailed, under a rubble of collapsed wall.

His lungs have healed and the chest tubes that protruded from between his ribs, draining secretions, are gone. His arms and legs are still in traction, with pins running through them, but his life is no longer in danger. The Engstrom is switched off and he breathes on his own now, sucking in air through the plastic fitting that remains in his throat. An oxygen mask hisses on his chest. He will go into one of the overflow rooms near the nurse's station.

The next two to be moved out are an elderly woman and a young man, both with classic internal bleeding from the spleen. At Shocktrauma, the young man's recovery is routine, but the older woman's survival is something her primary nurse is bragging about. Old people who are badly hurt are very apt to die.

The rapid admission of patients downstairs has a tertiary effect on the stepdown unit, which is about to receive the four patients from the CCRU. The stepdown unit, at this moment, has only three open beds.

That means a fourteen-year-old girl, whose legs were crushed by a bus and subsequently amputated by trauma doctors, will have to move. She'll go to the second stepdown unit around the corner, and then that unit, too, will be at capacity. One death is expected in the next few hours.

Until then, Shocktrauma is full.

The nurses and social workers are calling local hospitals and the better nursing homes, hoping to place a patient from the second stepdown unit. There are beds at University Hospital a few feet away, but the medical school will rarely allow a Shocktrauma transfer to take one of their beds.

From the beginning, the trauma unit's constant search for overflow beds was a major source of friction between Cowley and his fellow professors. The other doctors feared that the Shocktrauma unit might grow like some academic cancer, finally threatening to engulf them. Cowley had one thing right about his trauma patients: There were a lot of them.

Sometimes, in the summer, when it was motorcycle season and the roadways were jammed and it was Friday night in the city, and Cowley only had twelve beds . . . sometimes a trauma patient would appear miraculously in an empty orthopedics bed. The next morning the surgeon who was making rounds, and who'd planned to admit a patient into that bed, found a trauma patient there. He had to cancel his admission.

Worse, the professor was suddenly responsible for a patient Shocktrauma had dumped on him . . . a long-term patient at that. Trauma victims take forever to get well and, in the meantime, the professor didn't have use of the bed.

Since Shocktrauma patients generally have broken bones, the orthopedic surgeons were the ones who had this experience most often, and they complained to the chief of orthopedic surgery. The chief tried going to Cowley, but the bednapping continued. Finally he suggested that Shocktrauma should refuse to accept new patients when the unit was full.

Cowley was dumbfounded. Where would the trauma victims go? To the nearest hospital?

Finally the orthopedic chief took his complaints to the new chief of surgery, Dr. Mason. Dr. Mason listened and agreed. "If you are running a training program," the surgery chief explained later, "and you are depending on a breadth of different types of surgical problems, and all of a sudden you have no beds to put your new patient in that day... then your operative procedures the next day are cancelled, because the patient simply is not there."

Dr. Mason talked to Cowley, but it didn't help. So he restricted the transfer of trauma patients to orthopedic service beds. Cowley stubbornly refused to turn away patients. The midnight transfers continued.

There were other tensions, too. Plenty of them. The trauma unit's clinical director threw a medical school resident bodily from an operating room when the man refused to follow the protocol. It was considered polite for doctors, when seeking advice, to make the telephone call themselves... but when an admitting team leader wanted help, he was likely to send a medical student running to fetch the expert. By the time the student found the doctor, he was often too tired to do anything but grab the man's arm and start pulling. Cowley made a lot of enemies.

All the complaints went to Dr. Mason, who was supposed to be Cowley's boss. Dr. Mason reprimanded Cowley repeatedly, and felt insulted when Cowley ignored him.

Angry voices outside the university also sought and found Dr. Mason's ear. He reproached Cowley in writing for quarreling with Johns Hopkins officials. He ordered him to talk to no public officials without first notifying him, as chief of surgery, in advance.

Dr. Mason was especially concerned about how Cowley was conducting himself on the regional health planning committee. That was the group that was bogged down in an attempt to devise an emergency medical system that would respect the established medical fiefdoms. Cowley, Dr. Mason complained, was being quarrelsome. Soon Dr. Mason, instead of Cowley, attended those meetings.

His position severely eroded, Cowley and his team had nightmares of Shocktrauma's destruction. If Cowley were fired, as was beginning to look likely, what would happen to the system? In the hands of more traditional doctors, it might become the kind of place where doctors consulted over patients who weren't dying while the ones who were went to the nearest emergency room.

Cowley began calling the governor's friend, DeFilippo, in Annapolis. Something bad was going to happen, he said, pleading for help. DeFilippo reassured him.

"I kept saying don't worry," DeFilippo said, explaining that the governor had okayed a plan to make Shocktrauma a separate institute. That would mean that Dr. Mason wouldn't have the power to fire Cowley. Cowley wouldn't work for Dr. Mason any more. DeFilippo thought it was a neat idea.

"The governor had said, yeah, go ahead and get something drafted . . . but the legislature was in session, and we were busy. Meanwhile, Cowley and Liz Scanlan are calling me every day, and the whole damned bit. . . .

"I told him . . . I said look, doc, why don't you forget all this shit and go out and practice heart surgery and make three hundred thousand bucks a year and have a yacht in the Caribbean?"

"I don't want that," Cowley replied.

In the meantime, drafts of the executive order that would free Cowley from Dr. Mason had begun to circulate. Inevitably, someone made a copy, and somebody else made a copy of that, and in a matter of days the impending action was common knowledge in the medical community.

"The shit hit the fan," DeFilippo remembers. "Everybody was upset about it." Doctors and leaders of the volunteer fire departments seemed unanimously opposed to the order. The state medical society called its emergency health services committee into session to complain.

The most common charge was that the move was political, and that it would break a long tradition of political non-interference in university affairs. DeFilippo was indignant.

"Doctors engage in what I call politics of prerogative . . . like everything else, it is a question of ego. If there were any politics at all, they were being practiced by those doctors at University Hospital.

"I'm telling you, I spent four months on this thing, and I've never seen anything as political as this, believe me."

Back at the university, Doctor Mason ordered Cowley to take the chief of orthopedic surgery along with him on any meetings with the state's bureaucrats or politicians. Later, Dr. Mason would remember discussing the possibility that the orthopedic surgeon might make a fine clinical director, or number-two man, for the trauma unit.

Cowley, of course, already had a clinical director whom he liked very much, no matter who he tossed out of the operating room.

The lines were drawn. In mid-February of 1973, Cowley received a cryptic and anonymous warning, delivered by John Ashworth. The message was: *Beware the Ides of March.*

Cowley scowled at his chief administrator. What the hell was that supposed to mean? Ashworth said he didn't know, but it came from someone he trusted.

No, he would not say who.

Was it someone in the department of surgery?

Well, yes, said Ashworth. And he would say no more.

Cowley worried, and as he worried he called De-Filippo, and when he wasn't calling DeFilippo, he agonized over the bed problem. At Shocktrauma, beds are always something to worry about.

Meanwhile, Freckles knows that if there are many more admissions, Larry could have to move out to make way for a sicker patient. Strictly speaking, Larry no longer needs the womb; he needs intensive care. That is available in the overflow unit or, for that matter, at any good hospital.

When Larry gets to the overflow unit, his parents will visit and, presumably, they will tell him about his sister. Earlier today, Freckles tackled that problem one more time.

She didn't make the telephone call from the island. Trauma patients, with nothing to do but listen, often develop acute senses of hearing. It isn't unusual for them to overhear, and understand conversations on the other side of the CCRU. The nurse-chairman's office was vacant, so she used that.

Pulling the telephone toward her with one hand, Freckles dug with the other in her purse, extracting her cigarettes, lighter and a black felt-tipped pen. The letter came out as an afterthought. Toying with an unlit cigarette, she opened it and read it again, slowly. She put the cigarette aside and picked up the pen, instead.

As the telephone rang, she drew a stamp-sized box in the lower right-hand corner of the letter. Inside that, she drew a smaller box, and a still smaller box. After ten rings, she hung up and dialed a second number. Larry's uncle answered on the second ring and promptly handed the phone to Larry's father.

For a minute Freckles sympathized with the man about Linda. Larry's mother wasn't doing very well, and was taking sedatives. The pen drew another box and, inside it, a smaller box.

"Look," she finally said, "it'd be easier for you, for him, for everybody if you'd let me tell him now. He's constructing a world in which Linda is alive, and that's fantasy."

"Linda isn't dead yet," the man reminded her. "Until God takes her, she's alive."

The felt-tipped pen drew a large YES across the letter, then began thickening the "Y."

"Still," Freckles said, changing tack, "It would be easier for you, too."

"It's not something a stranger should tell him," the man said. "We have to be there, to pray with him, to ask God to forgive him."

Freckles put down the pen and reached for the cigarette. While Larry's father waited, she lit it and inhaled deeply.

"It was an accident," she said, "not something deliberate. I don't think you need to make him feel . . . guilt or whatever. Frankly, I'm worried for his mental health. He's suppressing."

The man had hesitated, and Freckles leaned into the telephone, tense.

"I don't know . . . " the man said. "Maybe . . . "

"I think it would help," Freckles said, encouraging. "I think he needs to know. I think he wants to know."

The father was quick. "I thought he was asking."

It was Freckles's turn to pause. She watched the cigarette smoke curl upward. "No . . . " she said, slowly. "Not lately. He asked at first, and when I fuzzed it up he got combative. He hasn't asked since we discontinued the Pavulon. That's what worries me."

"No," said the man. "I don't think so. If he's not asking, don't tell him."

Freckles argued, but it didn't help. When the conversation ended she hung up the telephone, lit a new cigarette off the glowing ember of the old one, looked at the newly-lit one, grimaced, stubbed it out and reached for the letter.

"Please advise us of your decision by or before March 20," the letter says. The director of nursing's name is neatly signed at the bottom, inside one of Freckles's free-hand boxes. Time is running out. Freckles refolded the letter carefully and put it back in her purse, along with the cigarette package and the pen. On the way back to the unit she slid the purse under the couch in

269

the nurses' lounge. She was in a hurry. There was work to do. She had to get the farmer ready to dive.

It is an hour later when the nurse trainee stops by to get a report on Larry. She will watch him while Freckles is downstairs in the chamber.

"I guess you heard," the trainee says, hesitantly.

"I sure did," Freckles replies, smiling. "When do you leave?"

"The end of next week. I'm going to an intensive care unit; I think I'll like that better. This isn't really my thing, I guess."

Freckles says she doesn't think it's anybody's thing. "We all leave sometime. That's the way this place is. It uses you up. Sometimes it takes three days; it took me three years. I think I'm used up. I don't blame you." Methodically, Freckles recites Larry's vital signs and recent medical history. The nurse trainee makes notes.

"You looking for a job?" the trainee finally asks. "You sound like it."

"Sort of," Freckles says, looking up from the patient record. "Actually, I've got an offer. An emergency room. Supervisory."

Freckles watches the trainee's face carefully, but the woman's expression doesn't change.

"I think," Freckles says carefully, " . . . I think I might be . . . I think I could be of some value."

"I bet you will," the trainee agrees. "After three years in this place, you ought to make a dynamite emergency room supervisor."

270

35

THE HEAVILY SEDATED FARMER LIES NEAR THE
end of the chamber, an oxygen mask over his nose and
mouth. At forty-two pounds of pressure per square
inch, gases thicken and become heavy and the patient's
chest labors slightly as he breathes. Freckles watches
him for the restlessness and irritability of incipient oxygen intoxication.

On earlier dives, a doctor came along, and the breathing was done by the respirator. Then, when the *C.
perfringens* still lived in the flesh of the farmer's hand
and arm, the foul odor of rotten meat filled the chamber. Today, there is almost no smell.

As she moves around the inside of the chamber,
Freckles is careful to make a minimum of noise. The
thick air carries sound like water, and a hemostat
dropped on the steel floor echoes painfully. Her patient
has tiny holes in his eardrums to equalize the Pressure
if he forgets to swallow, but he can still hear. After
three years, Freckles is still sometimes startled by the
trauma patient's acute sensitivity to sound.

The patient's half-dissolved hand and arm are exposed to the air, and Freckles inspects the tissue. The signs of gas gangrene are almost entirely gone, and the plastic surgeons will take over soon. The limb will be misshapen, but it will function.

The monitors, a fire hazard at three atmospheres, are outside. The sensor lines from the patient plug into a metal box near the head of the bed and the readouts are displayed on the chamber master's instrument panel. Freckles has to peer through the porthole to check them. The heartbeat is fine. The pressure is fine. Everything is normal.

"HOW'RE YOU DOING IN THERE?" asks a small loudspeaker on the wall.

"Everything's fine," reports the nurse. The pressure distorts her voice, raising its pitch and introducing a chirpy quality. On their first dives, conscious patients are sometimes disconcerted by the cartoon-strip voices of their doctors and nurses. The farmer is used to it by now, but, out of habit, the nurse speaks as softly as she can.

Outside, the chamber master paces in front of the floor-to-ceiling control panel, a communications headset clamped over his ears. In front of him, the pointer on a platter-sized depth gauge rests on the number sixty. The pressures inside the chamber are equivalent to those found sixty feet below the surface of the sea. Overhead, a time-lapse clock approaches the hour mark. A telephone rings.

Inside the chamber, Freckles looks up from her patient. "Okay," she says toward the loudspeaker, and reaches for a yellow phone. It's Tex, and he needs help finding Larry's parents.

"Linda arrested a few minutes ago. I promised I'd call them when it happened, but they don't answer the phone number in the chart."

"I know where they are," says Freckles. "They're at his uncle's house. I've got the number, but not here."

"Where then?" Tex asks. "I want to get this over with."

Freckles hesitates. "Okay," she says. "It's in a little pink book in my purse. It's listed under Larry's name, under 'L.' The purse is in the lounge, 'way back under the couch. You'll have to reach for it."

"That's a strange place to keep a purse," Tex says.

"Look," Freckles says, smiling into the telephone. "I'm doing you a favor. You want the number or not? And say, do something for me."

"What's that?"

"Put in a pitch for me. Tell them her brother has a right to know. He worries me."

Back at her patient's side, Freckles scans him quickly for any pressure-related abnormalities. Finding none, she presses a stethoscope against his chest, listening to the lungs work. Looking at her wristwatch, she counts his breaths. Twenty a minute. Normal.

Finally, she presses firmly on the thumbnail of his good hand, squeezing the blood out of the capillary bed beneath it. When she releases the pressure, the thumbnail is white, but the blood flow turns it pink again, instantly. All is well.

Glancing through the porthole, Freckles assures herself that all the monitor readings are normal. She moves

273

automatically back toward her patient for the next chore and suddenly, halfway to the bed, she stops. There is no next chore. She is caught up.

There is a chair in one corner of the chamber and she sits heavily in it, stretching out her legs. The sound of the farmer's heavy breathing is magnified by the chamber's closeness, and the thick steel walls shut her off from the outside world. She lets her arms hang limply at her sides. Her lungs, too, are tired.

Freckles jumps when the chamber master slaps twice on the side of the rounded hull with the palm of his hand.

Tex's face, pressed against a black telephone handset, appears at the porthole.

Freckles walks across the chamber and picks up the yellow phone.

"Did you get them?" Freckles asks.

"Yeah, I did. Lucky me. But I didn't give them your message. I don't think it would have been a good idea."

"Tough, huh?" says Freckles, watching the face.

"Tough. It was tough not to suggest they file a malpractice suit. I'd talk to the uncle about it if I didn't think I'd get run out of town."

Freckles looks at him carefully through the porthole. Her squeaky voice and the thick glass add an uncomfortable distance to the conversation. "Malpractice . . . sure, they ought to sue. But it probably wouldn't hold up. Usually in cases like that the hospital was practicing standard care, and that's enough. The best thing for you to do is try not to think about it."

"Is that what you're going to do? Just not think about it?"

Freckles's eyebrows go up. Not think about what, she wants to know.

The eyes watch her coldly through the glass. "And you had me thinking you really gave a damn about that kid," Tex says.

"Linda?" Freckles asks, confused. "She wasn't my patient. If you mean . . . hey, what the hell kind of remark is that?"

The surgeon's hand appears at the porthole, holding the letter. Freckles can't read the typing through the glass, but the large black "YES" is clearly visible.

Her face reddens. He went through her purse. *He went through her purse.* That's what he did!

The nurse keeps her voice low and even, glancing frequently at her patient, but the pitch moves from Donald Duck to Tweetie. On the other side of the curving chamber wall, Tex listens silently to the tirade.

"If you expect an apology, forget it," he says when she's finished. His voice is belligerent. The chamber master turns from his gauges to look at the young doctor.

"It'd be awful hard to miss a nice letter like that. Fancy stationery. I wish their medicine was half as good as their stationery. You're gonna love it there. Lots of carpet, lots of chrome. Good money. Maybe you can get your conscience chrome-plated with all that extra money. Whattaya gonna do, tell that little boy his sister's dead and you're gonna go to work for the sons of bitches that croaked her? Jesus!"

"Just a goddamned minute," Freckles squeaks into the yellow phone, but Tex is gone. Through the porthole, the dot that traces the farmer's heartbeat moves normally across the screen. Slowly, Freckles turns back toward her patient.

"Now what in the world was that all about?" she says.

"I was just going to ask you," the loudspeaker replies.

"I dunno. I'm sure going to find out, though. He's gone, huh?"

"Yeah, and he threw a piece of paper down on the floor. I can't reach it now, but I'll get it for you in a minute. Anyway, it's time. You ready?"

Freckles checks her patient once more, and satisfied, gives her permission to change the pressure. Outside, the deafening roar of escaping air fills the chamber room and echos down the hallways.

The nurse stands with her hand resting lightly on her patient's shoulder, her ears popping and snapping as the temperature plummets and an icy fog fills the chamber.

36

THE TALL BRUNETTE IN THE BRIGHT BLUE UNIform parks what appears to be a sheet-covered stretcher alongside the bed, then removes the sheet and false top. The tray is underneath, and it cranks up to receive a corpse. Cranked back down and covered with the false top and sheet, the morgue attendant could push the body through the main lobby without attracting a second glance.

Trauma nurses have removed the tubes from the girl's flesh. The electronic dot moves in a straight line across the screen, high above the still, dilated pupils. The stitched-up belly is sunken and Linda's left hand lies curled atop her right breast. Her partially open mouth reveals a row of small, even teeth.

The morgue attendant drapes a huge paper sheet over the tray, then pulls the girl's wrists together and ties them with a loop of gauze. Another loop fastens the ankles. The body slides awkwardly onto the tray, leaving behind a wrinkled sheet stained with rings of dried body juices.

There is a commotion on the far side of the island, and the attendant stops her work and goes to investigate. It is an arrest in bed six. A doctor heaves on the chest of a young black man while a nurse frantically fills a hypodermic syringe from a small pharmacy bottle. The morgue attendant absently scratches her arm as she stands for a moment, watching the drama before she returns to her chores.

A tag with Linda's name on it goes on the great toe of the right foot. Then the tissue paper is wrapped around the body and closed with adhesive tape; the tray is lowered, the false top is replaced and a sheet goes over the cart.

As the morgue attendant pushes the body out of the unit, the nurse shoves the syringe into the arm of the man in bed six. Above the patient, the electronic dot begins to bounce erratically.

By the time Freckles arrives on the unit, the resuscitation team is standing tensely by the bed, watching the dot and the dials. Freckles, throwing them one glance, walks directly to cubicle three and stops. It's empty. But the patient record is still there.

The nurse snaps the record book open and digs through the thick sheaf of papers until she finds what she's looking for. For a full minute, she stands in the empty cubicle and stares at Community Hospital's tastefully designed logo at the top of Linda's transfer note.

She closes the file with a soft click, looking up, through the glass partition. Beyond the glass, a short nurse Freckles doesn't know moves around an old man with a distended belly and yellow skin.

278

"Well," she says to the glass, "nobody told me. But then again, I didn't ask."

She drops the worn letter into the trash can, atop the tangle of soiled tubes and bandages.

37

ON FEBRUARY 26, 1973, COWLEY WAS SITTING BE-
hind his desk with the door open, arguing on the telephone. Outside, his secretary, Sandy Bond, stopped
typing and took the white envelope from the courier.
For a long time, she looked at the envelope before
slicing it open.

She smoothed the letter out on her desk blotter. It
was from Dr. G. Robert Mason, the chief of surgery.
It was very formal and very specific.

Carefully Sandy refolded the letter, inserted it back
in the envelope and put the envelope under her telephone. As Cowley continued to argue, Sandy typed a
few more pages of a long and boring research grant
request. Then she drank a cup of coffee, toying absently
with the envelope until Cowley hung up the telephone,
stomped through her office and disappeared down the
hall. As he passed her desk, Sandy slipped the letter
under her blotter.

When Cowley returned, the letter lay in the center

of his desk. Scanning it, he recognized a date: March 15. The Ides of March.

In concise and imperative language, the letter instructed Cowley that the Shocktrauma unit was a division of the department of surgery and, as such, would in the future be administered by Dr. Mason. By March 15 Cowley was to turn all payrolls, requisitions and contracts over to Dr. Mason's office. From that day forward the chief of surgery would manage the unit, including hiring and firing "of whatever nature, whether faculty, fellowship, house officership or personnel."

Years later, Cowley stares at his palms and, as he remembers, his voice subsides. "Y'know, I was so goddamn gullible. My religion teaches you to love your neighbor. . . ." he shakes his head.

"Well, I figured I had three options. I could resign. I could give in and stay. Or I could fight."

As the news circulated, individual members of Cowley's group drew together. The conference door closed quietly. "I kept remembering that warning," says Cowley. "Beware of the Ides of March."

A subsecretary distributed copies of the letter. "We were confused as to exactly what it all meant," says Liz, "but our reaction was to stay and fight."

Sandy dialed Frank DeFilippo's number while Cowley tapped a piece of chalk on the top of the conference table. "This is it," Cowley told the governor's press secretary. "They finally did it. . . ."

After he hung up, the group sat around the table and surveyed the danger. The atmosphere was funereal. DeFilippo had promised them the executive order establishing a separate institute and freeing them from Dr. Mason, but, on second thought, who was De-Filippo? A press secretary. And did the governor have the authority to intervene in the workings of a state university? And if he did have the authority, could he afford the enemies the order was certain to make?

Privately, Liz watched Cowley and remembered the things he'd done, the lives he had saved. And now his unit might soon belong to someone else.

"I couldn't understand how somebody who had worked so hard, and had dedicated himself so completely, could be destroyed along with all he had built . . . with the strike of a pen. I could understand if he were incompetent, but to be so competent . . . to have done so much, and then to be struck down just like that!"

Later, when Cowley was finally alone in his office, Sandy went in and closed the door behind her.

"He had a chair. Just one of those straight chairs. We knelt down at the chair. He prayed for God to do whatever was right and whatever it was, we would try to accept it.

"But we hoped that He could see what Dr. Cowley was trying to do, and know that he was doing it not for his own glory but because he really believed in the concept, and he prayed that right would win out.

"He started to cry. I don't know if he cried because I was crying or . . . I don't . . . we prayed out loud. And we cried."

In the meantime, in Annapolis, DeFilippo recovered from his surprise. He'd grown accustomed to Cowley's premonitions of doom, and a lot had been going on.

The legislature was in session, and he had been busy as hell. He'd told somebody to draft the order and then let it slide.

Mason's letter gave Shocktrauma until the Ides of March, but Cowley's panic had spread to DeFilippo. "I shot down the hall and I said I got to have that goddamned executive order before five o'clock today, that's it, period."

When the order was written, DeFilippo took it immediately to the governor. Mandel read the words quickly, signed, and handed the order back to DeFilippo. Now, DeFilippo relaxed.

Frank DeFilippo is a political technician, and when he does someone a big favor he hand-delivers it. It is part of the service. So on the afternoon of February 26, 1973, he didn't phone the unit. On his way home, he stopped by Shocktrauma and placed the order personally in Cowley's hands.

The executive order created the Maryland Institute for Emergency Medical Services Systems and separated the trauma unit from Dr. Mason's department. It allowed Shocktrauma to survive and prosper the way the now-aging heart surgeon from Utah had envisioned it.

Resistance remains, particularly in Cowley's own university, but with the passage of years the animosity is fading. Younger doctors read Cowley's scientific papers on time and perfusion, and see the logic. Today, when a multiple trauma patient arrives in a suburban hospital emergency room, it is often the emergency department chief who picks up the telephone and dials SYSCOM's toll-free number.

In 1980, the SYSCOM dispatcher sits at the center

of a complex web of medical specialty centers. Johns Hopkins University maintains two such satellite units, one for pediatric trauma and the other for eye injuries. Burn patients go to a burn center at City Hospital and premature babies are treated at neonatal units at City, University and Hopkins hospitals. Patients with crushed and mangled extremities, instead of going to the nearest hospital, are taken directly to microsurgeons at Union Memorial, which specializes in reconstruction and reimplantation of hands and feet.

Seriously injured adults and teenagers go to intermediate-level trauma units at Peninsula General on Maryland's Eastern Shore; Prince George's General and Suburban Hospitals near Washington D.C., and Washington County Hospital in Western Maryland. Critically injured patients go, as always, to Shock-trauma.

Perhaps most important of all, a steady stream of trauma residents and fellows come each year to Shock-trauma to study under Cowley and, when they leave, the young surgeons often take Cowley's convictions with them. Across the country, veterans of Shock-trauma are fighting the same battles Cowley fought, and for the same reasons.

Almost everywhere in the country, even today, accident victims continue to go to the nearest hospitals, and people are still dying.

38

THE PRIVATE CADILLAC AMBULANCE PARKS NEAR
the service entrance to the hospital, behind the trash
dumpster. The two blue-uniformed attendants pull the
empty stretcher out the rear doors, then lean against
the vehicle and enjoy the balmy spring evening.

Inside, in a small office, Larry's mother and father
listen intently as the doctor explains that their son will
have to spend at least a month in Community Hospital.
He will eventually recover, but it will be a long and
difficult process.

"I want you to understand," the doctor says. "I can't
be too forceful about this, and I know the psychiatrist
has already told you, but I want to tell you again. Your
son feels guilty about Linda. You've got to understand
that suicide is a possibility. He's going to require intensive psychiatric care, beginning now."

Larry's mother dabs at her eyes with a handkerchief.
The father looks cornered.

"I don't know how we'll afford it," he says. "We

didn't have very good insurance. It doesn't cover that sort of thing at all."

The physician understands the problem. "But your son pulled out his tubes, several times. He bit the stitches out of his lips. After he found out about his sister, he became profoundly uncooperative in his treatment. A broken mind is as important as a broken back . . . psychiatric care is going to be absolutely necessary."

The father nods. The mother cries quietly.

The parents are gone by the time the ambulance crew pulls the stretcher into the overflow wing. It takes half an hour for them to collect the records and make a pass at the Oriental nurse who hangs a bag of clear liquid above the boy.

When he's moved, the boy cries out. The nurse ties his wrists and ankles with strips of gauze.

Freckles stops the stretcher as it approaches the elevator, and kneels close to the boy. "Don't be so hard on yourself," she whispers, touching his hair. "Come back and see me when you get out of the hospital."

Larry stares at her without recognition.

Two other nurses hold the elevator doors open as the ambulance attendants roll the stretcher out, the bottle swaying above the boy's head. The stretcher bumps the door gently and the boy whimpers. Freckles watches until the elevator has closed.

Throughout Shocktrauma, loudspeakers click on. "THERE WILL BE AN ADMISSION IN TEN MINUTES."

Postscript

ON NOVEMBER 1, 1979, TEN YEARS AFTER Shocktrauma opened, the Baltimore City ambulance service abandoned its nearest-hospital policy. Trauma patients now go directly to one of four designated centers and the most serious of them all are automatically taken to Shocktrauma.

ABOUT THE AUTHORS

Joe Franklin won the 1979 Pulitzer Prize for feature writing. He also served for eight years as a journalist in the U.S. Navy.

Alan Doelp is vice-president and managing editor of PressNet Systems, Inc., an electronic news service. He lives in Baltimore, MD.